Infamies

The Notebooks of St. Valentine

BLUE CAT LIBRARY
KEENE, VIRGINIA
2011

Book Design by Silver Cat Works
silvercatworks.com

ISBN 978-0-9833142-0-2

Foreword

During the most recent fortissimo of San Francisco libertinism, just before the plagues of the late twentieth century, I periodically ran into a handsome South American visitor known only by his meat-market nom de guerre of "St. Valentine".

He generally wore the fashionable lemon-zest persona of the lightheaded bisexual, and though his reading came to light in increasingly fragrant remarks, he never mentioned any literary work of his own. Creative distinction was for others; outside the secret world we were the hollow men, neither hammer nor anvil; work did not mean your screenplay, or your therapy, or your marriage; work meant frugal speculation in commodities, securities, property, gems, art objects, punctuated by nondescript corporate employment during droughts; work meant congenital sinful failure of solidarity with the prosperous working classes.

Had golden youth permitted me to focus more sharply I would have tried to extract a proper biography, but this might well have alienated him. Though you would never have called him self-effacing, and though for another man his precarious independence and animal magnetism might have sufficed for happiness, part of St. Valentine had obstinately resigned itself to nonentity. The discretion with which his personal core evaded scrutiny even during that infinitely indecent time seemed to owe more to Nature than to intrigue, but the notebooks tell a more complex story.

My most vivid picture of him is in aesthete mode, incongruously perched in the uncharacteristic venue of the self-consciously earthy and leftish Petit Cafe on Russian Hill, thumbing through a Schumpeter from the shelf of marital aids for a presumed race of coffeehouse intellectuals, wistfully rattling off a dozen curve-fitting algorithms that left the long-wave cycle just one more unknowable thing-in-itself, saying creative destruction was just one more treadmill, it would rationalize dumping an ever-increasing mass of workers on the back of the State until the last capitalist owned the one machine that made everything everyone wanted, the rest would chop his (her) head off out of sheer pique, and the entrepreneurs would have wasted their labors vindicating poxy old Marx, except that by then the proles would all be overeducated overconsumers anyway, there would no atmosphere left to fight over etc.

When death called the loan on St. Valentine he was lucky enough to spend his final illegal months in the care of a long-suffering but politically enraged boyfriend on the East Coast of the USA, where chance brought me as well not long before his death on 13 July 1986. His living decomposition was a nightmare out of the Large Sutra, but lucidity had not yet given way to dementia. We discussed the subtle ways vice and virtue masquerade as one another, the politics of pleasure, the hazards of tampering with the mechanisms Nature has created to fool us into creating the dramatis personae of the next generation, the tyrannical veto with which biology laughs last at all attempts to abolish repression, the hydrogen bomb which eventually results from treating the Sixth Commandment as a kind of Fifth Postulate.

To my surprise St. Valentine thanked me: to his mind I, the token straight, had turned out to be a fellow traveler through the nth purgatory, and he wished me to have his notebooks. The gesture was supremely personal, tinged with humiliation and hellish remorse, and I doubt he would have forgiven me for publishing them even now, when the privacy of the confessional has given way to the global gut-spilling social media of herd individualism. He would have wished at least to reorder his fragments and to clarify some of his ironic postures, such as his baldness in reformulating the wicked political principles of antiquity. He was intrigued by the simian workings of political skullduggery, the jackdaw certainty of the con man, the elated greed and blood lust of the duped and cuckolded hordes, the cartoonish evil of the ancient tyrants; but instead of psychopathic will to power he had only his mixed feelings about the Church, his wonder at the biological improvements comically slathered atop our botched infrastructures as if to deny evolution any semblance of unidirectionality or progress.

Remembering the disastrous self-approbation of Elisabeth Förster-Nietzsche I have left the mass of reflections, maxims, notes, aphorisms, characters in the order I found. I could not begin to reconstruct the order of circumstances that inspired them, and all the mutual acquaintances I can think of are dead.

Lovers of the fragment tradition reaching from the Presocratics and Theophrastus will find scattered homage to the French moralists, Chesterfield, the Jesuit, the great Italians and Germans. Mathematical conceits a la Lichtenberg and Kraus underline St. Valentine's psychedelic religious conviction that we are cross-sections of arbitrary-dimensional entities. There is sardonic lament over the tragicomic grand-strategic errors which provoked Persia into overwrought alienation; and anger over the prosecution of private mental states as heretical deviations from the orthodox wickedness of military Keynesianism. There are moments from love affairs wildly out of tune with California days. A mishmash, private and uneven; but though it is not properly random, capricious collage is apt enough given St. Valentine's endorsement of Maurice Pope's heroic attempts to modernize the stochastic appointment methods of Athenian and Venetian democracy.

Well, have fun if you can, I'm off to check out the bardo. -- According to one of its spluttering enemies, Islam rewards the faithful with seventy Virginians; but St. Valentine plumped for the Tibetan afterlife: you can make the sublime mistake between every pair of their quadrillion worlds.

JM

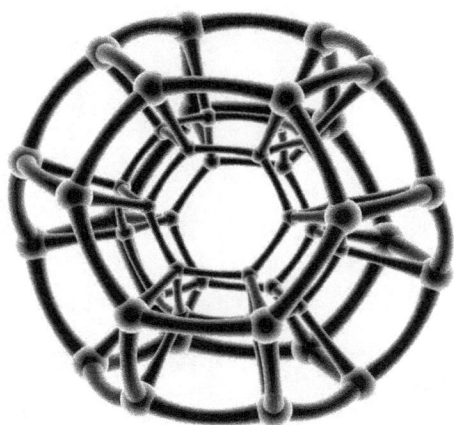

Artistic and religious lies are the foundation of culture because life demands we divide 10 into two parts whose product is 40; it can only be done with imaginary numbers.

Someone satisfied with the approbation of fools must somehow admire them.

The salesman dependent on the whims of his spendthrift customers considers himself more autonomous than the student dependent on loans, the smoker dependent on cigarettes, the unemployed violinist dependent on government relief.

The person who checkmates us often did not mean to.

Greater and smaller men can relate as a number to its negative, with the ratio the same no matter who is on top.

Our punishment for vanity is misleading feedback.

Modesty is a preemptive strike on malice.

When constructive change introduces itself with a surgical knife we can mistake it for a shiv. This is useful to gangsters. Also useful to them: often we can feel an obstacle but not see it clearly enough to name it.

Celebrity actresses are imperial courtesans to the tyrant of the majority.

A large X cuts a ridiculous figure in a series that converges only for fractional X: a petty post, a dull conversation.

Addiction is other people's habits.

There are jungles where the most brilliant man will be poisoned straight away by flowers any local fool could tell him are deadly.

Only complete secrecy of alms frees the receiver from the anxiety of keeping silent about our flaws.

The view that all voyeurism is a political act equivalent to rape would amuse a dog watching two other dogs on a street corner.

Transmigration and infinite-dimensional Heavens and Hells show the Divinity more poetic respect than do one-shot lives and rewards. Higher-dimensional entities manifesting as discrete beings credit him with a more colorful Creation than do isolated souls. Nothing more need be said about the preposterous notion that persecuting Persians has something to do with the advance of civilization.

Holding a fortress well beyond disgust and despair for the sake of someone who cares or deserves much less than we realized.

Disciplining oneself at chess does not make one a virtuoso pianist.

Chipped blue chips: social outcasts driven below their intrinsic value by herd passions. Christ bought up every share in the scapegoat role the others fled.

Incompetent imitation is the most offensive form of flattery.

Sheer surprise can make a bad character genuinely grateful for your foolish trust.

Our inner tormentors create facts to foreclose our options.

Premature worry attracts calamity as tennis dress attracts tennis partners.

In despair as with burn wounds no touch is friendly.

Renounce most everything that appeals to a contemptible enemy.

A great library contains the best that the best men have ever thought of saying. How can anyone unable to find respite from boredom in a library hope to find it in the conversation of chance acquaintance? -- Through a pheromone rush, silly.

Perfect contempt closes the wounds of age and bitterness.

Detective work is simultaneous equations.

Resorting to hackneyed authority to conceal an unwelcome originality.

You despise your enemy yet you are surprised he would ignore intellectual defeat. You are astonished that an abstraction like justice is not the sort of music to soothe even an animal mind.

In reality the object of her envy had long since forgotten the sensation of victory.

Checkmate and disaster are more interesting than the torment of nothingness.

Sexual inquisition by the State poisons the heart, so elites will eventually find a way to flood everything with sex and store everything for inquisition.

The art of retreating from argument.

Many elections and promotions assume a good follower is the best leader.

Better brain scans will finely distinguish between honest indignation and lust for the sinner's advantage.

She noticed that her dupe shared some of her own virtues, whose market value her victory was depressing.

Society's minor dissimulations accumulated until he found himself integral to a clique of total strangers.

How long has mankind been able to afford the distinction between quality and quantity?

Pity the master of an unpopular viewpoint.

The great man was sad to detect flattery in someone who had been proud enough to abjure it. He remarked how many married couples go twenty years without learning each others' tastes, how tricky it can be to find your dupe's ruling passion.

Proponents of the Market and the State are equally eager to infiltrate and pollute private life. Beijing and New York both end up with a microphone in every flowerpot. "One dollar, one vote" ends up a Politburo.

Forcing someone to submit to your point of view means writing yourself a loan against his account; someone will eventually buy and call it even if he never manages to.

The affair overripened suddenly, like a peach in a heat wave.

Perfect social grace is the intuitive ability to deduce analytic expressions for the intersection of minds, like the curve formed by an ellipsoid and a sphere, or their hyper-cousins.

Let the first favor be an accident; its successors will have the seal of safe custom.

Theoretically a sublime genius could show which sort of mediocrity would please the greatest number of solvent people. Everyone reasons from the possibility of the demonstration to the presence of the genius.

Abandonment of long-cherished schemes offers our vanity greater tax advantages than we imagined.

Seasons when all our allies retreat for different reasons, falsely suggesting the common cause is abandoned.

The one occasion you decide to be really aggressive will be the one that falsely paints you a sadist.

Aging and graying are the slow falsification of a biological conjecture.

Politics is the art of undersampling, neurosis of oversampling. Neurosis samples the world so finely that it never completes the data sets it would be perfectly capable of filtering.

Often the trends that appear to have left us hopelessly behind are merely stabs in the dark.

Classified ad: "this position is the perfect vehicle for unconscious masochism".

Someone bumped into him from a surprise angle and he spilled her secret all over his trousers.

Everyone gets an occasional moment of detached clarity about the absurd insatiability of everyone else's desires.

No one is free enough from perversity never to challenge truly hopeless odds.

To be rid of her he consistently slandered her admirer until she regarded adultery as an intellectual triumph over his pusillanimity.

Since the data of life are infinite, affirmation of life is incoherent.

She succeeded in seducing a powerful enemy into misplaced contempt; then her hubris seduced her into thinking they would never reawaken to the threat. When they finally ferreted out her strengths they also found terminal illness.

Rotation through our ordinary space reduces a higher-dimensional object to garbled fragments; incoherent events and personalities can conceal an exquisite order fatigue despairs of discerning.

Habitual criticism of weaker men smacks of cannibalism.

A copy survived at the Mulla Firuz Library only because three centuries earlier a thief had used it to cover up the absence of a priceless tome on remedying impotence with ground elephant tusks.

Even an evil single-mindedness is rare enough to attract endless admirers.

A distinction that cost a lifetime can be instantly undone in thought by any beggar.

Eventually we will be able to recreate the exact mix of hormones triggered during a brilliant thought, and conversely to produce reflections electrochemically. We will become annoyed at brilliance just as the ladies did whose spinal anomaly made it impossible for them to walk across a room without having yet another orgasm. Perhaps the idiocies of the pharmaceutical Inquisition are preventing a tragic glut.

To paranoia everything is raw material, never finished product, however extravagantly this compliments the intelligence of real or imagined enemies.

The need to compartmentalize means something is wrong; something is always wrong.

One of the things we will read in the great book of life is the list of dangers we were saved from before we even knew they existed, by people who scarcely seemed to exist.

Cunning defenses of beloved unfairnesses carry venereal diseases of the mind. Seeing the telltale intellectual sores, one can forget the victim had every reason to expect safe sex.

Withdrawal from competition is a form of public service.

Ask a 'postmodernist' whether he knows enough calculus to have attained the seventeenth century. Ask a specialist whether anyone can ever really escape the nineteenth.

The treadmill of other people's malice would be a great workout if you could be certain of the off switch working.

Occasionally someone sleepwalking through life will astonish us with a half-lucid remark to the effect of "Curious how I walk even though I am fast asleep."

Find out who influences the person at the center of influence.

The Divinity ought to send an angel to point out: "all right, five minutes from now will be the best moment of your life", or "you will look back at this and wonder why on earth you did not slash your wrists when you had the chance", or "My dear, this is the very last chance you will have to begin anew."

To disrupt an enemy's mind, pair him with someone who combines his positive and negative ruling passions.

Will-to-power philosophy ignores poisoning of the will. Pride can be diseased rather than merely camouflaged.

People can so successfully conceal their feelings that we are shocked to discover they experienced the lack of our company as a frustration.

The sophist was offended at the thought that he might be satisfied with mere victory rather than money.

The greatest embarrassment is underestimating someone else's virtue.

The vector that threatens us from below is the rocket eastward in someone else's reference frame.

Temporary depressions are the muscle soreness of a productive workout.

The magic moment when you must first decide whether you are willing to impinge on someone just because you can.

Poverty, chastity and obedience are doubtless listed as psychiatric disorders in the American Medical Association handbook.

Perhaps when Christ suggested giving it all away he was in the same mood as the trippers who jumped out the window saying they might as well go to Europe.

Asceticism forces the organism to bake its own bread.

Never poison your enemy's wine on your first drinking bout or first communion.

Half of what passes for therapy is just encouraging clients to externalize their ego costs.

Manipulation of the masses is intellectual pedophilia.

She infuriated the buffoon with gracious ironic adjustment to the trivial technical problem of his social milieu.

When a man has truly given up on something it is as if he had already been through the horrors of a bad marriage. If he is not too scarred, granting his wish at this point maximizes our satisfaction because the disillusionment taxes he has paid up front will not be hovering to sabotage his gratitude.

All historical eras are always alive. Feudalism in the corporation. Banishment through vetting.

Poisoned self-love has a detachment that can see the future, read minds, and hopelessly distort everything else.

Moral pride is the desire to capitalize on a lack of desire.

Love that would have made an idiot of someone else also made a photographic negative of the fool.

An infinity of flattering strategic rationalizations for our successes, like the infinite restatements of mathematical theorems.

The propagandist despised the intellectual for leaving the hindbrain to its own devices.

Properly suspended judgment can be a severe handicap in a superstitious society. A fraudulent oracle with a thirty percent success rate is cheaper than a mathematical model with 20 percent.

Why does insulting someone's intelligence feel more profound than insulting his tastes, which involve his entire nervous system?

Illicit drugs are said to loosen family ties and undo economic conditioning. According to the Gospels this is supposed to be the job of the Church.

The test of honesty is renouncing an illicit advantage you deserve, knowing you will be scorned as a fool and will scorn yourself.

Justice is too much bother.

Most people are thoughtful only because they can afford to be.

All ages praise shrewd adaptation and all dream of an unchanging paradise.

Stoicism has discovered that we would be less cancerous without our tumors.

Denial wants to be paid as courage, obstinacy as dedication. Everyone wants a raise.

Not realizing the effect was deliberate, they had kept on applying a Kalman filter to his 'capricious distortions' until the message was degraded to chaos.

Rationalized laziness is shrewder than failed virtue.

Not all suspicion, not all resentment of hypocrisy is projection. A prison cell is a block of concrete, not a neurosis.

An aesthete getting by on the smashed narcissism of a beggar. As a business executive he would have had the lowest overhead in the country.

Untested virtue judges sinners more cruelly because it views temptation as a stroller on deck views a whale five miles off.

Opulence overheats the imagination until we can never again be satisfied by anything but unicorns.

Disease is a commentary on something around us.

He teased her about a contradiction that did not exist; she let it go in astonishment that Nature had so conveniently blinded him to her actual inconsistencies.

Mathematics could not have progressed without people crudely treating irrational numbers as rational, divergent series as convergent.

She was more indignant at his escape from justice than at the fruits of the escape; then she realized it was her whom justice would have condemned.

Despising scraps of paper and bits of metal is not philosophical, but that does not mean despising lucrative errors is unphilosophical.

Positive roots of life's equations call the negative and imaginary roots charlatans.

One chapter in the secret book of life is the autobiography of the person most wasteful of opportunity.

Real love of justice requires neurotic checks on egotism.

A man under constant threat can make his disguise as unconscious as a woman's.

Burst asset bubbles are the menstruation of Fortune.

The clandestine service devised a camera that would make the target population's driving license photos the most demoralizing ever.

Medicine that fixes anxiety and depression also helps many to feel okay about genocide.

Vulgar wisdom. Everyone can win the lottery simultaneously if they work hard enough.

Vulgar wisdom. Once you know your leg has been chopped off, you are well on the way to growing it back.

Shame at dead love is mathematical. We took a few curves and crudely projected them out to infinity.

Love and friendship are fickle where the ego is at best a slender majority.

Forgiveness is when you stop caring.

Intellectual honesty resents the low overhead of the dishonest competition.

The desire to improve ourselves is the desire to make ourselves into something different from what pleases our friends.

We suspect not our friends but the fate that made them false, that spoiled our confidence in our judgment.

The most trivial existence would be a better mental grindstone than the most towering philosophical monument if it did not typically go unused.

A lukewarm reputation sets off good works like a cheap setting for a good stone. A dreadful reputation lends them the fascination of a bag of cash found at a dump.

We want people who came to us in need to act like they came in want.

Feminine modesty conceals charms and defects as merchants conceal margins.

Everyone wants their lens to be the standard grind.

A pleasant clown, constantly praising himself for indecent virtues.

Perfect equanimity: grinning as a monkey reaps idiot admiration for an idea he tore away from you.

Coarseness always has the option of dragging delicacy down.

She delicately lowered herself into his trap, concealing her skeleton key in the lock.

There are false premises only stupidity can guard against.

The perfect thinker would have to cope with the entire civilizations of the ancients and moderns. The closer this comes in practice to coping with infinity, the more random the distinctions between overall grades of knowledge, between politics and a rigged casino.

Not everyone deserves to eliminate the middleman.

Many a capitalist is as superstitious as an Indian pariah when it comes to the theory of karma. Let him carry his superstition to its conclusion, and invest his karmic triumph transmuting himself into an angelic orb rather than buying yet another murder license.

Mobs mistake hot streaks for congenital decisiveness.

Announcing your entire intent matches you with the entire range of your enemy's straw men.

Perhaps the Jewish habit of jabbing one another with indiscreet questions started as a kind of military exercise.

She reproached herself for not speaking her mind, forgetting that it would have exposed her to savage injustice.

If psychiatric ills all had physical symptoms many people mocked as neurotics would instead be mocked as amputees.

Injustice can vary directly with self-righteousness. What beats the joyous self-satisfaction of a political lynch mob?

He advised the poor young woman to make powerful men dependent on her.

When hope disappears it takes with it the memory of how it came to delude us.

Underemployment stultifies; technology exacerbates underemployment; what was I just saying?

Someone caught unawares may wrongly assume they lack the strength to resist a dangerous passion.

It speaks very poorly for many deities that one is supposed to expend half one's energy rejecting the snares of their pernicious Creation, and that one only gets to perform miracles once one regards their worlds with the perfect contempt of an old geezer contemplating a luscious whore.

She thought her compatriots would admire her for freeing herself from the national vice.

Automation has changed the requirement of constant work for fame.

On this one occasion it was her brains the lady wanted pumped; his manipulative questions reaped poisoned knowledge.

He thought the voters might finally be bored enough with everything else to try out intellectual superiority.

Scorn of laziness is loudest in natures assured of reward for effort; scorn of affectation is greatest in natures demanding credit only art can deserve.

The vilest malice feigns intentions it would be dishonorable to question and candor it would be tasteless to attack.

Improved communications always pretend they will give the Muses a dowry but those girls are still naked.

Intellectual insects are immune to high doses of radiation.

Words like 'miracle' and 'spiritual' warn so clearly of fraud to come that financial loss may be the victims' secret goal.

All he had left in his closet was a dinner jacket and gold pince-nez, and the only place he could afford to live was with friends too rich to care.

Privacy invasion is rape; technology revives the droit du seigneur.

She infuriated him by constantly raising strangers' expectations of him to infinity.

Mediocrity in its bay wants excellence floundering on the beach.

Tombstone: "Anon, grandmaster at ego chess".

It would certainly be convenient if intellectual immortality came the same way as biological.

The spirit of an age is a lock requiring both truth and falsehood to open.

Too much great literature can collapse the veins like too much heroin.

Slander is hard to kill because it stimulates the imagination to a long line of implications; killing many takes longer than killing one.

Her arguments were moons eclipsing suns.

Overcompensated people naturally overrate zero-sum reality; the stupider among them may be partially sincere in their mystification over a poor man who prefers the tyranny of his imagination to the tyranny of someone else's agenda.

To earn the suspicion of uselessness, display a conspicuous ability to destroy idols.

Rescuers often enter on an irrelevant vector. Direst straits relieve you of the overhead of mistrusting this.

The carrot is mightier than the stick but there are not enough to go around.

Ability to inflict suffering is not the same as moral superiority; the softness of the belly is not a virtue of the knife; yet he thought the sudden silence of the opposition made him an intellectual.

Countless small acts of neglect may converge to the sum of desertion without convincing us we are entitled to the punitive damages we badly need.

There are serious moral errors that make us as beloved as harmless intellectual errors.

Sometimes real discretion simply invites projections of vulgar criminality.

Gracian sums up the moral tone of the Jesuits exquisitely in his admonishment to flee the unfortunate, i.e. to have a memory lapse about Christianity.

People too weak to forego institutional approval like to believe outsiders beneath understanding the virtues of institutions. People too cowardly to take a risk like to believe those who take it are beneath understanding the concept of risk. Hardened cuckolds like to believe themselves superior to the puerile illusion of fidelity.

A primary symptom of neurosis is compartmentalization, the foundation of the national security state, where polls document neurotic trends, elections are neurotic vindications and morbid dependency and aggression mock one another's intellectual inadequacies. Fortunately neurosis is not a real disorder but a poetic fancy of our illiterate forebears, who lacked happy slave pills.

Some lies can only be backed up with further lies their authors would be above telling in isolation.

Building the upper stories before the basement is not always imprudent. The real number system had no logical basis until the nineteenth century.

The jury is always out on the largest political ideas.

The more brutal a ruling ideology, the more proof it claims itself entitled to demand from opponents.

Bright young activists do not understand how seriously they threaten those living from lies: how many people can survive every distinction between getting and earning?

A communist is someone who denies the infinity of wisdom in parties to contracts.

The world's second oldest profession: the frame game, exploiting everyone's resentment at being cheated of his glorious destiny. Manufacturing conflict between enemies, and executing one as the author of the other's murder. Sending moralists to chase heretics, or disgruntled colleagues to foment discontent, or robbers to be arrested at the murder scene they thought was a jewel heist. Sowing dissension over an inheritance, or convincing sons they have been disinherited without warning because adopted. Convincing a woman a poison is the aphrodisiac that will fix her marriage. Poisoning her party meal. Overdiagnosing disease. Leading neighbors to blame one another for property damage, or for their wives' imaginary adulteries. Tempting borderline types into pimping, counterfeiting, drug dealing. Bumping off cultists during weird rites. Photographing johns with whores dressed as the queen. Convincing political opponents that the king has gone mad and they are free to laugh about it. Convincing officers that the king is angry with them, or that they have been implicated in treasonous treaties, payments, gifts, sabotage. Fingering defectors as having left families behind in the enemy's clutches.

You buy and sell a picture. It turns out to have been stolen several owners before you. You have performed the same labour as if it had not been. You must return the money to the heirs. This morality does not apply to huge tracts of stolen land.

The sixth commandment is a Zen koan: never poison pleasure with betrayal.

Even innocent information had to be suppressed in this context.

An obsession is an infected mental wound.

Rewarding mediocrity, ignorance, even laziness is Fortune's idea of wit. Fortune favors the bald.

They agreed that he would play the sentimental hero and she the airbrushed slut.

Prudence is an unchristian virtue.

Some wits speak in algebraic equations to people who only do arithmetic.

The moment we discover the ineradicability of a habit is a moment of death. The belief in future time is the belief in the flexibility of the personality.

Excessive information does not always paralyze the will; it can force impressively random action.

In the secret book of life there exists a general formula by which we could discover what sort of knowledge is destined to moldiness. Literary work that has escaped the confines of its century probably stimulates different hormones than hackwork dying with fleeting passions.

Nature must regard some of our more inadequate theories as slander.

All truths reduce to tautology, but the distance between the reality and the formula creates as striking an effect of added value as the length of a mathematical proof.

Lechery is the lust of the unappetizing.

Without victory determination eventually dies and with it complacency eventually destroys.

Everyone is a champion at some nonexistent sport, and most minds are broad enough to grasp their intractable flaws.

Our century was compelled to atrophy the sensation of outrage.

The imagination is cruel to provide so much pleasure without the culmination of happy madness.

Some people who complain about the atomization of society deserve it.

Watch for the unsubtle hint that reveals your reformer's information about you to be fragmentary and illicit.

Decoy weaknesses can cost so much energy to cultivate that you might as well have let them find your real one.

Human craft is shallow enough for superficiality to command a greater sum across multiple economic niches than depth across one.

We have a whole arsenal of deadly weapons we cannot apply because all minds wander. If you could constantly view everyone you met as an idolater you could constantly control them.

Often the last vulgarity to go is fear of vulgarity, or revolt against that fear.

Steadfast defense of truth would be easier were she not always spitting on us.

Having the strength to recognize and avoid a waste of time is worse than useless when vital acquaintanceships are at stake.

Which success will be our final step to hubris?

It is easier to discern someone else's main talent than one's own.

Barbarians sense when they can force an unearned answer to a rude question.

Careful plans are scales and arpeggios.

Huge swathes of the body and the mind are in the pay of enemy forces. There is a free way to leave their treachery behind: turning waking life into a lucid dream.

A thesis on commercially motivated ephemera takes as much brute work as a thesis unifying electromagnetism and gravity. A comfort to admirers of brute work.

Her mind was a handsome leather-bound dictionary with false definitions of every lucrative term.

The difference between people is less the quantities they see than the operations they interpolate between them. One favors addition, another division, another exponentiation. Sometimes two people will impose exactly the same combination of operations but beginning with different terms; each finds the other's result absurd.

Without the simian wish to distinguish oneself good theories would rarely be tested and improved any more than bad.

Something in us has died when we achieve indifference to the pseudo-intellectual triumph of a wicked adversary.

In the life of the intellect as in economic life most of the great fortunes go to the distributor or broker rather than the manufacturer; this is why the most fashionable books are often overgrown magazine articles, graphic tabulations of the figures from yesterday's trading on the intellectual stock markets.

Two liars bludgeoned each other into switching positions.

He was hemorrhaging, true, but not from their kick in the testicles.

For purposes of persecution socialism was the same as communism, and what purpose was there other than persecution?

By demanding immediate proof of aliens resident on earth she triumphantly refuted the idea of life on other worlds.

An adversary attacking distortions of our positions startles us the same way as someone demanding our wallet. The vulgarity surprises us so much that we forget the ample resources we have to defeat and disarm him.

Moral relativism. Calling someone's mind "fried" is a scholarly compliment in the Vedanta, meaning that evil tendencies in the unconscious have been seared like roasted seeds so they cannot reproduce.

Fortunately the lies that could undo his adversaries were consistent with the contemptible principles they were sworn to defend.

He was far enough ahead of the times so that even he could not believe what he had written, and destroyed it.

Never assume your opponent cares to distinguish between his interests and the truth.

Anti-intellectualism: a scalar resenting a vector. Ideologues: a mob of vectors mocking a coterie of tensors.

Genius is accompanied by melancholy because greater imagination augments the capacity for disillusionment.

The insensitivity of a dullard is an achievement for a sensitive man.

The pressure of unaccustomed necessity taints what hours we are able to steal from it for mental work.

Cultural autarky would be a splendid ideal for a creature who could go without air for more than three minutes.

God has analytic expressions for all our series; charlatans gamble he will reveal them no matter how bad the sample.

One way to protect a child might be to insist it view everything as literary raw material.

Prudishness is the fallacy that a strong ratio of intellect to will can and should be extended to infinity.

A young man would have to be quite a scoundrel to intuit the extremes of feminine falsehood.

Everyone confuses his self-preoccupation with the inwardness of genius.

She censored her children to protect them not from vice itself but from envy of vicious success.

Collective fear masquerades as collective wisdom.

Many parents want the law to assume free will in the criminal courts but to regard their creation of extra resource claims as an inevitable fact of nature.

We are so weak that we reproach ourselves with inability to beat the philistines at their own game.

Art dealers expert in going rates regard failure to associate beauty and money as an intellectual inadequacy.

People will give you a surprising amount if they are sure it is not making you too happy.

The insanity defense is widely ridiculed, but how many laugh at the unconscious-hypocrisy defense behind the madman theory of deterrence?

Discontent is acceleration of our claims on life or vice-versa.

To a metaphysical idealist will is capital, genes unearned income.

The failure of hard work looks very much like the squandering of capital. With only five percent more capital she would have remained a respectable rentier rather than a spendthrift.

To revel in disillusionment, seize upon the most repulsive aspect of someone's character and watch him beam as you praise it to the skies.

Vanity would not be so easily wounded if one could know which misunderstandings and slanders would cause cash damages.

Knowledge grows exponentially, wisdom arithmetically.

Pride is vanity in a static arena.

The most complete fulfillment so far of Mill's views on the necessity for a free, equal partnership between the sexes is American womankind. Strife and war will be ceasing any day now.

Inferiority too is capable of avoiding overly familiar relations with its own kind.

Grasping the flaws of your national character is not a reversible step.

The comfort of knowing ostracism unearned is too cold.

Unearned income looks down on unearned indebtedness.

If we had invented our environment we could speak of earned income.

Mediocre writers have herd instinct at their inmost heart. Hitting the perfect average of your herd is as easy and as hard as picking the right numbers at a horse race.

The secret book of life contains the total number of hours worked by each man to pay for the pleasures of each other.

Worship of willful naivete is spite toward reason.

If the theory of natural selection is true, our fears and lusts will eventually come with properly refined probability estimation. No one will be afraid of heights unless their beam is breaking. All gifts will be evaluated in terms of the giver's net worth. There will be full disclosure on the expected value of sexual pleasure, and the race will stop procreating. Meanwhile let our enemies have every opportunity to taste the thrill of gambling.

For a complete picture of someone's material demands on the cosmos, ask him to define 'spiritual'.

The desire to rule is the desire to punish, and where all parties desire to rule, checks and balances never depart the sadistic realm. That can begin only when offices are filled at random.

Government by polls is jury verdict without trial.

Every dream fulfilled is a fresh revelation of the infinite non-self.

We think we envy the unfettered force of defective consciences, but imitating them gives us an appalling hangover.

Unless you pretend you wish to be master or slave, you can end up hated by both; vulgar people will despise you as intellectually unequal to the grownup task of fraud.

Even otherwise virtuous people will hate you if you manage to avoid the compromises that snared them.

She was not actively but passively sadistic; what aroused her was the thought of spoiling it for the other.

Incompetent flattery dotes on petty virtues, stresses mutual acquaintance with unappetizing associates, lavishes useless gifts, promises benefits that repulse the conscience. It insults us by assuming our position is our fulfillment.

Who has never seen the cruel and stupid smugness on the face of a new convert to an unjust majority?

Waging secret war against you from envy of advantages irrelevant to your heart's desire.

The world calls (2 x 3 x 5 x 7 x 11) a wondrously complex personality and (1555 x 2777) a shapeless anomaly.

Successfully anticipating markets can require a more than abstract immersion in collective mediocrity and folly.

People who disbelieve in altruism have never been awed by a friend's destruction.

The world is ruled not by Satan but by Judas Iscariot.

Raw human nature resents rejection even from people it has perfect reason to despise.

Little girls and boys at play: which will be the first murderess, the first adulterer?

Broad-based ownership of securities and real estate assures permanent rivalry amidst the lower orders.

If she knew how little he cared about her flaws she would despise him for failure to share her neurosis, so he acted mildly fed up with her imaginary inadequacy.

Why does one not wish to return even to illusions that were clearly net benefits?

True lust is as rare as true love.

If we could always choose any brain state we wished, would we eventually diddle ourselves into the tedious adventure of everyday life? This is what religious people say God has done to us, or done as us.

Creditors, believers. They believe that others will believe. This is what the old moralists said of women, running with the pack, choosing lovers on herd consensus, speculating on a force which appears to overwhelm the credulity of others. If men chose mistresses the same way, Hamlet would be aroused by a long brothel queue.

The goddess Fortune resents inability to forget the difference between virtue and reputation.

Where does flattery soothe more, on temporary accomplishments or permanent flaws?

In American politics Jesus is a rentier.

Your first circle of defense should be females, the more obstinate and unjust partisans; your second the eunuchs, dwarves and hunchbacks who would perish without you.

The ideal role for an enemy is leading a doomed revolt in some province stupefying enough to atrophy his abilities.

Supreme adaptive mastery includes preparedness for all sorts of suicide.

Hostile takeovers create foreign kings.

The Hindus think the self just water wings for meditation.

Disease repulses by underlining the absurdity of human will.

Find the secret passage from the shrine of a labyrinthine personality.

Choose someone who tolerates rather than loves secrecy: they are less fascinated with the drama of betrayal.

A perfect plot damages only the relevant aspects of the victim.

If the egotism of mankind were bounded it would not casually endorse the mathematically infinite ratio between positive and zero net worth.

Each generation thinks the gratifier of its desires has the worthiest fortune.

Overly casual nudity is passive aggression, swamping the erotic reflex.

Philosophical genius is knowing what is worth disputing.

Reasons for imposing secret tests can never completely obscure their sadistic impetus.

Many ancients regarded 'service industry' pricing as intrinsically fraudulent.

Bad teachers convince us the only things worth doing are those we have no gift for.

A beautiful vehicle rusting for mere lack of fuel.

When one person urges you to follow another, ask yourself if they plan to share your money.

Psychotherapy is exorcism; society considered as an oligarchic company store effectively charges the patient for daemonic possession too.

Economic embargo is the tribute the fraud of one nation pays to the force of another.

Propagandists instill pride in the luxuriant growth and pearly whiteness of cuckold horns.

Satan's finest hour is convincing us we have found a villain evil enough to legitimize illegitimate retribution, the "death after false accusation" routine among the ancient Aryans and perhaps still so among the monkeys.

To force someone into a damaging alliance, capitalize on their moral self-image by presenting false evidence that their enemy has been falsely accused.

Discretion is the patch over a gouged eyeball. The man never trapped by impulsive trust may be as imaginary as the yogi who walks on water.

Journalists were awed by the fluent foreign languages of a diplomat no longer able to distinguish between truth and power even in his native tongue.

Winner-take-all is the law of nature, proportional representation the law of civilization.

Minds combining our ruling passion with irrelevancies cause the mental analogue of postcoital disgust.

The disgust of being unable to lower one's price for fear of giving less placebo satisfaction.

Buffoons imagine art prices are fixed in some vaguely official dimension, like the going rates for milk and missiles. You can buy a book that says what to pay.

The young woman stated with staunch confidence that in a democratic republic critics of the government's foreign policy were free to choose between exile and house arrest.

The world wants us to trade real work for symbols.

Anixus believes all taxation is unjust. His customers came to him along a road; surely the road grew in the meadow, like a tree; it maintains itself, like the air; why should anyone pay for it? Why should anyone ever pay for the use of anything Anixus does not own? Zerpes is at the other extreme, imagining his authority to collect taxes implies an ability to write intelligent laws.

Sarcasm makes its target's position seem not just unearned but random.

Merit means money likes you.

What bothers people most about forbidden drugs is not the crimes of users but the sincerity of their contemptus mundi. Their minds wear Sabbath costumes after others have changed back into chain mail.

Ripe corruption is indifferent to the truth or falsehood of reasons for anger against it.

Don't bother conquering countries you don't want to live in.

No integer is the sum of more than nine cubes or 19 fourth powers, but you would not know it from some resumes.

An academic who refused to believe literature would be desiccated by the increasing abstraction and purification which fertilizes mathematics. He boiled away the differences between plots and situations until the paltry handful of tropes looked like the dried palette of an amateur painter.

Know when to feign peace. A neurotic may give away the store in vindictive triumph over the prodigal son blushing with the rouge of feigned shame and false conversion.

Many people would be saints if anyone else were. Corruption delights in virtue's inability to hold its breath indefinitely. Sometimes the victims end up feeling sheepish about ever having bothered to hope life might be more than servicing of random desire.

Mothers must also worry about good influences on their children. Criminality can be nothing more than a determined attempt to rise above the banality of everyday life.

Reality is not necessarily an improvement on neurosis. Is tormenting yourself with illusions always worse than enduring real malice?

Art hints at a new organism.

Rage and hatred are photographic negatives of samadhi.

The science of the future may regard our experimentation as a farcical kind of undercover entrapment, too dull to grasp how crudely it is mangling its object.

Prejudice against illegitimacy boils down to love of money.

The Mizán ("Balance") of the thirteenth-century dervish Bakái Váhed argues that the energies of elemental matter conjoin until they become minerals and further adapt into vegetables and animals. Is this not ninety percent of what the average person understands today about Darwin, random mutation, DNA soup? When Váhed proceeds to tack on divine creation of mankind, does he not arrive at a cosmology palatable to many American school boards? In Váhed's world humans also routinely degenerate into a colorful cast of animals and minerals; what if, in the next stage of Darwinism, bad computer instructions cripple the egotism of the genes?

Naive women like to believe that because political battles all have nursery analogues they can all be resolved by nursery methods. But once in office they are not the calm governesses they imagined. One of the most conspicuous fruits of sexual equality legislation so far has been its reminder that girls commit mass murder too.

Covert action is the heroin of statesmen.

Even an atheist can see the comedy in a villain's willingness to destroy his immortal soul for a pretentious pittance.

Cripple anyone you cannot treat well.

A cunning plot only seems more complex than baking a chicken.

Incompetent pollsters send interviewers to the vintner with poisoned jugs.

States perform cruel actions to send a message to audiences that may not exist.

Any dirty trick you play on your enemy should first be played on yourself, though not revealed until he suffers; and on a random victim, to thwart generalization.

Sometimes the compliments of our dearest friends provide the most crushing openings against us.

In his own country the prophet is an intractable partial differential equation. In the new coordinate system of a foreign land he transforms into tractable ordinary equations.

After years of poverty on the road the musician had become so avaricious that even his chord progressions were based on compound interest series.

In a market where any idiot can prosper, what is to become of the non-idiots?

Shamefully obsolescent ideas are the most pleased to think of themselves as grand reforms.

Charisma is relative to the moral standing of the audience. A charismatic person is a blue glass mirror.

Never had there been such an opulent display of zero net worth.

Everyone else is an idolater, and most of their idols, being tailored to their ridiculous needs instead of ours, are by definition daemonic. They are all parasites on the State. More than likely their military service was a cover for treason.

Karma says every profit is really just a generous line of credit with continually rising interest rates and an enormous balloon payment.

Complete despair would be a recipe for invulnerability, but complete despair is physical death.

People praise themselves for the endurance and persistence of their most egotistical endeavors.

Most friendship and enmity depend on false inferences we do not discover in time.

Calm your allies by saying adversity will be brief; frighten them with the enemy's cruelty.

Proselytizing for detachment is a contradiction in terms. Until they have nothing at stake, most people will kill snakes one by one rather than burn down the house.

We are often disgusted to discover the true source of someone's confidence.

Faith is partly hope that the enemy will fall prey to the same confusion that mysteriously destroyed our well-considered plans.

He had only acuity enough to ruin the self-respect of a better man.

Society insists on providing endless motives for suicide and should also provide endless means. Prohibitions on suicide are arbitrary market distortions.

The ultimate source of her self-hatred was an unfair remark she heard about someone else when she was three.

Friends keep the threads of each other's lives together in desperate phases as the Hindu and Arab scribes did Greek mathematics.

People will never forgive you the loss of certain illusions. A teacher who insists children view things as they are insists they refuse the only thing powerful people want from them.

Everything worth knowing comes either accidentally or too late.

Where success is defined as mass appeal, liberal education is the same flirtation with failure as a heavy weightlifting set.

Superior generality defeated: vectors beat out quaternions by being 3-D arrows.

Sometimes the problem is not unwillingness to credit people's pretensions but inability to determine exactly what they are.

To understand the spirit of the laws, imagine a man who likes to slaughter game through his window. Occasionally the game will manage to nail a slot across the window at one angle or another. But there are always plenty of holes, and if the slats spoil the fun they are easily removed.

When people have committed a great injustice against you, you are sometimes better off if they kill you. Otherwise your existence may never stop mocking their pretensions; their cruelty will grow without limit.

Charlatans claim their algebra of personal relations can solve quintics and sextics by arithmetic and roots.

A spy whose thievery and blackmail has brutalized thousands announces in the newspaper that he cannot understand the vulgar mania for privacy.

Circular reasoning is the clue to injustice in paternalistic laws. The law is there to protect you from yourself, because if you break it, you will damage yourself, and if you do not, we will damage you to prove ourselves right. -- Our relative lack of damage is therefore a natural law.

Your virtue depends solely on the political convenience of parties unknown. An envoy was once sent to provoke an unpopular man into criticism of the ruling powers. At one point the man pointed out that science tries to isolate dependent from independent variables: a society's militarization may be dependent on apocalyptic threats from without, or it may not. The word 'science' was seized upon to portray him as a witless adherent of 19th-century "scientific socialism", a violent ally of dead Russian provincials. His joke about the "famous Karl Marx novel Moscow Show Trial" cinched the proof of his antiquated communist sympathies.

People want to take more money out of life than they put in, so an honest politician is an unrepresentative politician.

In a capitalistic information economy Christian education is a finishing school for hypocrisy.

The steps in a mathematical proof are jazz chord substitutions, layer upon layer until a Gregorian chant becomes a modern symphony.

Some lies are so huge and so vital to the happiness of so many that we end up hating the people who gave us the ability to see through them.

Half our Christians only venerate the personality traits Yahweh shares with Satan.

The world is a computer program no longer supported by the manufacturer.

I know something the other person does not. I end up with his money. Merit and reward. These are like cause and effect in physics; an economic Hume would doubt they have anything to do with one another.

Half the trouble and half the good in the world comes from the stalwart courage and perseverance of mediocrities; the balance is zero, but a shiny zero.

We convince ourselves that we are worth more to our friends alive than dead.

Serious opinion is divided on how to teach advocates of preemptive war the meaning of defenselessness. Schopenhauer and Russell suggest putting them under a waterfall, while Kraus recommends a public horsewhipping once a year for life. In America one could subject the matter to a vote using electronic implants in their brain stem. Those who agreed with them could remain silent while the rest could register protest by contacting them electronically, thereby triggering incontinence, or an epileptic fit, or a heart attack. One could judge their popularity by the number of microseconds it took to reduce them to a vegetable.

Most victories are Pyrrhic.

The inability to distinguish between money and truth is an incalculable advantage, like the inability to distinguish novelty from banality, because the colorblind pay each other for being sensible enough to ignore silly theories like color.

Struggle hard enough against banality and you will find yourself completely deserted.

Opposition to contraception and abortion rests almost entirely on the desire to drive ground rents up and wages down. The rest is the resentment of those once fooled into thinking there might be some other justification.

It must be a statistical anomaly that when I am asked to support the rights of women it is typically by some woman enjoying rights I could scarcely hope to share.

Why can there not be a political controversy involving principles less than twenty thousand years old?

It is far from obvious that cigarette smoking damages health more than newspaper reading.

Technology places logarithms in the hands of people who only know addition.

If the roots of action are as obscure as the theory of the unconscious suggests, all uses of time are equally suspect.

The real end of life is the day when we stop believing in an audience worth pleasing.

Some people say there is meaning and even immortality in the universe, to match their longings. Do they think there also exists a way for everyone to produce artworks as profound as those he can consume?

Indifference about betrayal is one of those stoic or Indian principles that would be perfect if only one did not exist.

Some pretensions we cling to only because we think our friends depend on them, and sometimes we are right.

The critical spirit splits a half-truth into a whole truth and a cloud of dummy missiles.

Life is a sore loser towards the philosopher who really succeeds in preparing for death.

The Divinity must be disgusted to receive our naive thanks for the opportunity grossly to abuse his creation.

The fast road from Christianity to Zen Buddhism. Loving your enemies and praying for those who spitefully abuse you is not strictly possible; it must be a koan.

A man wrote a book explaining why his book Nirvana was better than other people's chemical Nirvana. The chemical version was like electric lighting, which is not really lighting, since light bulbs sometimes burn out and they are not made of wax. -- Behold the rationale for more than a million jail sentences in this country, which fancies itself the most rational republic in history.

In youth we do not understand how great a blessing it can be that scarcely anyone cares about anything outside themselves. So many people would have done us in if their egos had not obscured our existence.

People sometimes bill art as a deeper mirror of things, but it is more like imaginary numbers in mathematics. A quaternion may not represent anything strictly real to us but after a few operations you get back to our space much enlightened.

Some people live great literature without ever realizing it. The grandiose resumes of others are dictionaries of received ideas.

Completely honest dealings preclude the subterfuge of arbitrage. As communications improve and eliminate middlemen other people will hopefully be held to a new moral standard.

She went through a puny crisis before selling her soul to the corporate world.

The nation had genuinely forgotten how it came by its assets and was outraged by the adversary's violence.

Authors with no idea of the immortal competition are among friends. Authors with a received idea of the immortal competition are among fewer friends.

Voluntary sterilization is a vote of no confidence in a world constantly upping the zero-sum stakes. Absence of children is constant proof that they are not some inevitable fact of nature justifying political services.

Anxiety of influence. The ancient Abadians, whose successors he proposed to exterminate en masse for their failure to appreciate enlightened "Western values", had embraced religious pluralism as an increase in the number of roads to God. Allah was Brahma and nothing else really existed. The only sin was cruelty. They touted the intellectual soul, the rational sciences, the calculus of probability, as the true fountain of eternal life. In all likelihood they had experienced every intuition that ever ran through the mind of Bruno or Galileo; the future their perfumed temples were getting at was Cal Tech.

Perfect liberalism requires a morbid excess of shame, perfect conservatism a morbid lack.

Neurosis is a necessary and insufficient cause of empathy.

A magic glass to discern willing women.

There are phases in life where gremlins might as well exist. If you try to be polite you are thought supercilious. If you succeed in being clever you are thought impudent. Every question asked you seems calculated to demonstrate some trivial weakness, and together they put you in a ridiculous light.

Some of the great thinkers give freely; with others you realize belatedly that you have signed a promissory note.

Debt is death, whether for the debtor or for the person his leverage trounces. Existence is debt.

Modesty is a problem when acute awareness of our flaws also keeps our virtues on the shelf.

A self-appointed authority on mysticism and philosophy said false cosmic consciousness was better without drugs.

Cats would be an even greater comfort if they would occasionally point and say: "It is -that- you are supposed to write down."

A morally unambiguous fight is such an exquisite rarity that many people cannot resist the temptation to fabricate one.

Marriages between people suited to one another only in some extremely crucial area of their personalities go through endless fights before what should have been a swift divorce. A semi-convergent series that oscillates in huge cycles before converging to a negative sum.

Aim to conquer centrally guarded powers and to attack them at the center. Fragmented powers mean never-ending battles.

Sometimes courageous defiance of received ideas causes torment from within. Our reason is strong enough for the adversary but it refuses to admit defeat, resorting to covert operations.

Insane economies of scale. A man comes into my office and calmly informs me that he is an associate of space aliens, that he rides with them around the galaxy, that they are planning to drop a huge comet on Germany and bounce it into Egypt.

Some ideas are fancy dress, others are earmuffs, others condoms. Militarists wear condoms as hats.

"Team spirit" is American for "soviet".

A security risk is someone who disagrees with your ideally imperfect market.

When we arrive in the afterlife we will discover the one torment that we all shared but no one could bring himself to mention.

Thanks to medical research he got an extra ten years to ponder the incurability of his disease.

Writer's block is when you have nothing to say.

Glib scribbling is the promiscuous sexuality of the mind. Four thousand orgasms down the road the partner has lost all identity.

He felt apologetic about having seen for himself how little she differed from the others.

The journalist bragged about his ability to fill an exact number of inches in record time. A master bricklayer.

What if there is selective advantage in neurosis? How would a dialectic of humiliation and vindication benefit a species while wrecking the individual organism? Neurotic competitiveness - more determined focus on some goal only partly visible? Neurotic withdrawal - random mutations of the herd instinct?

Public sex education is an oxymoron, like 'public domain trade secrets'.

He was thought unoriginal until he resigned himself to writing banalities.

Many things invite contradiction but few deserve it.

"Rent-seeking" is one of the economists' most evocative phrases. They use it to mean "demanding something for nothing", tacitly conceding that land ownership, really existing capitalism, is ultimately bogus.

We learn nothing from life. We vacillate between pride at enforcing fallacies, and shame at not living up to inchoate standards. We alienate those we could genuinely have loved and allow idiots to debase the currency of our affection. This makes death anticlimactic. Surely there was some secret, not just a snore and a corpse?

The satanic aspect of sexuality is its refusal to stay fixed, or its refusal not to. Love is not true unless it can withstand infidelities that would make us unworthy of it and vice-versa.

In theory you go to Nirvana and can then come back and play in the world, making everybody happy. In practice you get rid of all your particular desires and are left with general tension that leaves you useless to anyone.

He took her helpless goodwill for hardened spite.

We were better off ignorant of the potential vulnerability we had no chance of defending ourselves against anyway.

At the end of the list of profound authors the page is blank. They seemed to be instructing us in a method, then there was nothing left to apply and nothing left to apply it to.

Everything has too many implications.

The primrose path to solipsism. Much conversation has the same chance of competing with nicotine that a man has of competing with a vibrating dildo.

If you are always frank you will end up in the company of people who can withstand any criticism, or who despise you enough to regard even the truth as merely on loan to you.

The public loved the sheer scale of the straw man; how it burned!

He habitually insisted the geometry of life did not require a Fifth Postulate. Eventually there was not enough Euclidean space for a foothold.

You abstain from a shameful activity only to discover it was the only thing that made you attractive.

They started a war on behalf of people who did not really exist.

Politics is where bomb-throwers pose as sharpshooters.

Obstinacy insists on generalizing from the one exception.

Everything is a dream symbol.

Political power - the right to force other people to take play money.

Satanism is the triumph of power over truth.

Experience eventually ruins all pleasure by suggesting a desert for every oasis.

Blanket condemnation harms self-critical people most: they will waste time reviewing every possibility. With a boor you need specific allegations, and proof, and laws and prisons, since nothing else is likely to penetrate his complacency.

He boasted about his experience like a leper boasting about his flexibility.

The German language makes "surveillance attack" one word. Much of politics centers on who gets to invade whose privacy. One person gets to go on wearing silk and the other must go naked. A certain type likes to rip the skin off people's faces, pretending he is removing a mask. "Aha! Beneath all his pretensions there is nothing but scar tissue!"

The spy claims to have built the gun when he merely pulled the trigger. The warmonger decrees that rebuilding bombed churches is a better investment than fitting them for solar power.

Without anxiety there is no motivation to question everything.

Evil men have the strongest motivation to get control of the justice mechanism, since there is no limit to their claims on others and they stand to lose the most from objectivity.

How much genuine heroism springs from petty fear of being labelled a coward?

The motivation for framing someone as a liar. Why desire to deflate a nonexistent claim? There has to be some idea that a legitimate, threatening claim could be made. Some virtue is perceived as a threat. The bearer has to be found guilty of a sin. This must be something the accuser views as a sin, otherwise he would not likely perceive the possibility of its condemnation. The accuser must have a sensation of humiliation and wish to transfer it to another. Also the victim has sinned by implicit rejection of the need for extravagant claims. By not making them, by living without them, he denies that the claims would be interesting. The accuser needs to prove that the claims are worth making and that the person not interested in them deserves subjugation. It would be intolerable if the other were not interested in competition because the desire to compete would be revealed as inchoate aggression. What vindictive triumph is achieved by the neurotic who succeeds in a frame? The fantasy that his standards have a real basis, that his struggle is more than a psychiatric disorder. The other must be made to struggle, so that it can be shown that struggle is in the nature of things, not just a sick game. If it were a sick game the trophies would also be sick. If the trophies were sick, superiority would be spurious. If superiority were spurious identity would be lost. The frame preserves a false identity. It papers over an unbearable contradiction between reality and ideal. The longer the contradiction goes on, the greater the investment in it, the more unbearable the prospect of loss, the greater the incentive to frame. The interest payments mount on the pretensions. They approach infinity together. The only thing that could stave off bankruptcy would be total co-optation of enemy resources. But the enemy too is a sick projection.

Slander is exasperation at failed exploitation. The other refuses to be inferior. It ain't fair.

Someone who imagines himself entitled to executive authority over billions of people should be compelled to prove it by analytically resolving a differential equation in billions of independent variables. He will fail even with billiard balls, let alone souls. Perhaps he could run the neighborhood parents' association as a booby prize -- no, five hundred variables is just as hopeless.

Body and mind masquerade as one another.

Try to offend scattered minorities rather than organized majorities.

Perpetual peace depends on females losing their taste for murderers. Faites vos jeux.

The American Dream: to deserve something for nothing. Being as Deserving. If some people only deserve something for something, and others deserve something for nothing, there must be infinite differences of merit. If there were such a thing as an infinite difference of merit, how could a finite creature perceive it?

We three-dimensional creatures can project life into motions on a two-dimensional screen, but a screen of one dimension would offer us no hold at all. Dropping just two dimensions yields nothingness. What does this say about an infinite-dimensional deity watching our three-dimensional drama?

The world tries ever harder to stimulate desire and decision. If it succeeds, how much time can remain for fulfillment?

Should we advise young people to be wolves or prey?

Some thinkers are manufacturers, others stockbrokers, some both.

Try for what is highest. Olympian vision is highest. You are not an Olympian. Try for what is impossible. Be ludicrous.

Managing an economy means convincing people they need what others offer. Managing a religion means convincing people they do not need what the world offers.

The Bodhisattva has compassion for the nonexistent.

Religion says the other people's demands are always reasonable. Most people like to be the other people. An irrationally exuberant market where the stampede into the exploiter role leaves the exploited role undervalued.

The lads thought it would be funny to order goods on behalf of someone who did not want them. It would cause gratuitous expense and drudgery, indignation, and embarrassment for the merchant. They grew up to manage political campaigns.

Why would someone whose whole existence is dedicated to taking more out than he puts in, endorse a market perfect enough to clear?

Truth is a virus that fools the system by locking onto cells intended for illusion.

The Persians take too many poppies and prayers; we take too many consumer goods and love affairs and political crusades; who is more contemptible?

Parliaments are stool samples of public opinion.

The kind of success that embodies all the false strivings of its moment.

Scandal depends on the contrast between the prestige of an office and the vulgarity of the inhabitant. If there are enough vulgar inhabitants in a row the prestige and the contrast disappear.

Rape is would-be ravishment.

The editor was one of the few really worthy successors to Bierce and Mencken and Parker. His wit was like ice sculpture. If ephemera had not so attracted his attention he would have been an immortal, but he could not help himself from trading in the raw mass appeal of the buffoons who received his exquisite spite, so if his writings were the *Praise of Folly* you would have only two lines of text for every thirty of footnotes on justly dustly churchmen. He must have believed his admirers were really agents of the enemy convinced against their will. He insulted them, made passes at too many of their daughters and demanded money from them where others offered free space. Because he could deflate ninety percent where others could only manage thirty, he took it upon himself to deflate the other ten. He resented the gossiping spies who had long ago abused their power to deny his superior mind, but he could condemn them only in gossipy terms. Content to be far superior to people with five-minute historical memories, he opened essays with quotes like an undergraduate. His failure to step up to the roulette table of specific ideological remedies he justified with the realism of earning a living in the age of information, with routine nods to pluralism and the uncertainty of all change in an unknowable universe. His adventures in prediction almost invariably went astray, although he correctly anticipated the failure of capitalism to better the lot of the masses oppressed by pseudo-communism. He was forever plagiarizing himself, perhaps on the correct but unclean assumption that none of his bon mots got the circulation they really deserved. - The description of his faults obscures his more important merit as the leader in his generation of journalists, someone who would be a billionaire or prince in a more intelligent world, just right for a national medal.

He believed there could not be scientific laws of history. Such laws would change the society they purported to describe. But when a student of financial trends illustrated a generalization about the currency markets, he took the money.

Paying high art prices is often an attempt to buy one's way beyond a banal success.

The near-infinitude of pitfalls makes experience often just as worthless as intelligence.

A school aiming at perfect preparation for life would have to force excellent students to accept inferior grades and submit to patronizing lectures from other children who had not read the books.

Ideology is nuclear attack on civilian ideas.

People who think the sense of life is to establish a paying constituency appear to serve the present but never really leave the immediate past.

You double an investment equal to one percent of your debts. Your enemy makes ten percent on an investment that wipes his out a hundred times over. You have made 100% and he only 10%; he mocks you as a petty gouger.

Some political books are indignant that anyone should reproach them for openly admitting they seek to palm off zero-sum gains as mutual aid. Arguments as tampons.

One fact about an author can permanently alter the significance of an abstract work. He argued cruelly against the poor. He never learned the trick with women. And yet reducing authors to their biographies or physiologies is just barking over the superiority of our nervous system.

Where two copies of an artwork have only trivial chemical differences, the distinction conferred by possession of the original has nothing to do with the work.

Think of fraudulent exceptions to your opponent's rule.

Conventional resumes and conventional beauties inspire the same boredom as a series of perfect squares.

Egotism convinces us that we are alone not only in illusory virtue but in illusory sin; hence the relief of scandal.

Breathless ephemerality wants to pass for scholarship; vulgar astonishment agrees this would be mutually flattering.

The desire to be a serious museum of the present is a desire not to be a serious museum of the future.

Who is protected by a copyright on the work of an author all of whose immediate friends and relatives are dead?

His art symbolized arriviste desires to buy the works it imitated.

She saw aesthetic merit in opposing abuses long dead, but mocked indignation at current abuses as time wasted interacting with incurable vulgarity.

Collective cowardice knights itself prudence and affects pity for those outside its orbit.

Knowledge and talent are geodesics; money is the straight line segment through the sphere.

Bourgeois solvency judged it an appropriate rendering of deadly poverty.

Like a cat she had discovered that by pressing her trivial demands during an unrelated emergency she could increase their inconvenience – her significance – tenfold.

Investment grading of art is as anti-Christian as any other investment grading.

Every era makes advances in the science of vulgarity.

Vauvenargues was a very young man with the very old man's awareness that most drama comes from overlooking the obvious rather than discovering the spectacular.

Will will do almost anything to pass for intellect. Intellect returns the favor only when bankruptcy approaches

Treachery avenges itself if the traitor is capable of remorse. A thief with an object he would rather never have taken has a tumor: the consciousness of his inadequacy in the eyes of the law.

Abused children are said more likely to perpetuate pederastic rape, and some refugees create humanitarian disasters because their personalities secretly require the drama of the refugee camp.

Politeness towards a rogue can serve him as a pretext to defame your intelligence: you were polite, you refrained from presenting the detailed indictment, therefore your opposition is weak and sickly. This becomes tragic when the desire to defame comes not from the rogue himself but indirectly, from his gull, whom you rather like and whom he has successfully poisoned against you.

Circumstances forced him to feign idiocy as she smeared her sordid infidelities in his face, glorying in triumphant revenge for a betrayal that had never taken place.

Over-education takes the power of our abstract algebra beyond our ability to translate everyday occurrences into its variables.

There are moments when you can only pray the heart really does have some reason transcending your reason.

Building a home that required extra energy for heating and cooling became the mark of the beast.

Poverty unravels the tastes it frustrates. Become poor enough to regard nearly everything as unrealistic and you being to look like someone who was never courageous or clever enough to explore reality.

You would think reading a child the Old Testament would be enough to teach it that murder is the essence of society, that murderers prosper. But Biblical events are endlessly far away from a naively prosperous epoch; even the media are remote from the childish mind. It does understand you, though, if you say the main job of the President is to kill people.

The fulfillment of free-market economics is capital concentration sufficient to make a police state profitable. Ordinarily it is less expensive to manipulate desire than to maintain dungeons. But after compound interest has made the principal essentially indestructible, sadism can for some time indulge itself at will.

Before you do good arouse the fear you will do evil, to make the recipient doubly grateful.

An ancient astrologer who slipped up would blame the mistake on faulty astronomical data. The precursor of econometrics.

American militarism is the view that if your army is able to disrupt an opponent's operations then your economy builds better products. The dog who bites muscle from a man's leg is cleverer than a man, who would not have been injured if he had the sense to see protein in its proper light.

Vulgar sadism has the diabolical advantage of being stupid enough honestly to overlook the merit of what it destroys.

Nothing so bold as a woman caught in the act. With the equanimity of the perfectly void conscience she declared that her family's unjustified murders were not relevant to -- you know, whatever; that her lovely mind should not be soiled with the screaming reality of her satanic vileness.

Cultures are like neurotics, battling the suit worn by the old evil until it creeps up behind them in what they thought was high fashion.

Limited government would be automatic if there were percentage limits on the collective Schadenfreude content of public policies.

History shows that a critical mass of fools can always maintain its fallacy long enough to starve the virtuous opposition.

Male and female desire are the same series but transformed for different rapidities of convergence. The male error is to go straight to the analytic expression and the female is to dwell on infinitesimal terms.

Neurosis is a false courtroom mocked up by a hostile intelligence service.

Vigorous deceit sneers at exhausted honesty.

Political debate is forever assuming the existence of integrals. Missile defense, universal employment -- if you can write them they can be integrated.

To build an enormous constituency in your lifetime it helps to subscribe to the most vicious lies of your era, but there are so many to choose from.

Admit only a premise that you can twist to a conclusion opposite to your enemy's.

A scientist too dispassionate to notice the corruption of his funders.

Politicians who have tasted murder begin to tout the higher morality of murderers.

The inventor gives his soul, the imitator someone else's: guess who has lower overhead.

Is it greater maturity to outgrow covert methods or to outgrow hope in democracy? True belief in covert action is permanent renunciation of the scientific ideal.

Washington completed the dialectical synthesis of Nazism and Judaism: Holocaust Museum for me, Holocaust for you. All that remained was to drop the pretext that the market was something different from the Reich. Like history's sad goodbye to Venice and Athens.

Unfair advantage #2222: the inability to grasp the contradiction between advancing the ideal of gender equality, and murdering or prostituting foreign women.

She bungled the order of integration and arrived at her true love soaked with the karma of unworthy rivals.

Just a few more murders and they could afford to be honest. Just a few more adulteries and they would find true love. Just a few more frauds and meritocracy would rule the earth forever.

The unconscious rage of Nietzsche at the ease with which mediocrity gets to comprehend the futures markets just by projecting its own limitations.

The most popular temporary tattoo: the mark of Cain. In Washington, DC they like it enough to make it permanent.

The worst manners is thinking of one person while sleeping with another, but other people's bad manners can come in handy.

Conspiracies make you a hostage to fortune.

Capitalism says you earned the interest on your grandmother's fortune but someone else earned the lack of interest on your great-great-grandfather's.

Some truths you can only grasp when you are ill or grumpy, since a completely happy organism has no incentive to change.

Murder as therapy, as maturity. Hitler's invasion of Poland was immature; Poles were not really oppressing Germans. Our lies are nobler, and our killers are wittier in calling themselves animals. We are beyond adolescent indignation at murder and character assassination, which we know are as commonplace as shoplifting.

Salesmanship is the belief that counting on good faith is a sign of stupidity alone. Rapists too must pride themselves on shrewd awareness of human nature.

There are characters so evil that only hatred perceives them accurately. You may hear them preaching against hatred, since without it they would get off scot-free.

Late 20th-century America discovered a hitherto unsuspected connection between herbs and the anal nerve, and called it justice when a man was raped in a dungeon for consuming a plant.

He professed himself shocked and disappointed by the fruits of his unethical surveillance methods, legal only because of deliberately unconstitutional legislation. They had altered the victim as a cyclotron alters the delicate atom.

A new truth can be as repulsive as a fetus and its abortion much less troubling to the average conscience.

Adult courage includes the courage to ignore spiteful withdrawal of interest.

Hatred too is a thought experiment.

The velocity of money depends on reproductive conditions God has now seen fit to place under our control.

The greatest power would provide exhaustive lists of crimes and proofs before dropping bombs.

Lichtenberg's differential element is the infinitesimal remainder of an interesting intellectual sensation as it vanishes into banality.

The ingratitude of children is proverbial but the ingratitude of parents can be far worse. What sort of brain scan could measure the work performed by a child keeping a horrible secret for life?

Memory can shock us with the vividness of supposedly erased recollections, and with the impotence of the vividness.

The different pillars of self-confidence look the same from the outside. The man who has lost an arm and a leg does not understand the man who has had both eyes gouged out. Is two not two?

A nasty thief picked at the keyhole to old wounds.

Either one is saved, in which case the rational thing is to proceed to heaven as fast as possible and leave the salvation of others in more capable hands, or one is damned and all of existence is just one nightmare or another dreamed by a sadist. Russell probably said the prohibition on suicide was invented by creditors and dependents.

Youth is the illusion of free will. To understand life you have to be damaged beyond repair by something supposedly well within your control.

The golden rule stopped her from saying she loved him; she was applying it for the benefit of a third party, but he misunderstood it as coldness and incomprehensible ingratitude. The loss of this sincere love was a terrible blow for her, but he was content to walk away both from her and from the other people they had hurt. Then she discovered what had inhibited her all along: he had been sent to her as a disgraceful practical joke.

They told themselves all was fair in love and war but it was obvious to everyone that they were the war.

Sometimes we appear to mock others' misfortune when our real bottom line is sadness and pity; this is easy to forget when the tables are turned.

People who have committed murder must tell themselves they know life better than the innocent. What else are they going to tell themselves?

The fool's advantage is going straight to the stupid conclusion instead of tormenting himself with intelligent alternatives on the way.

Refusal to believe it is too late is a secular Pascal's wager.

If there were a God he would forgive an honest rationalist before a selfish speculator in mercy, but not before the speculator had the dishonest enjoyment of his psychological insurance policy.

Society needs glass prisons for snoopers.

Brain recordings will make certain cold manipulations of intimate emotion actionable, even capital.

Aphorisms are a lottery. Most of the combinations welling up in the mind are time wasted, then comes a minor jackpot.

Arriving immediately at a closed-form expression, she had to endure the taunts of those who clung to numeric approximations.

Anything we can comprehend and admire in another author is an accessible phase of our own system.

We enjoy some strokes of wit the way we commit adultery with our own wives, passionate for the beautiful woman in the new gown.

Almost every mortal offense we give is unwitting, something we would happily retract even had it been meant as it was taken; while our most hateful attacks so often give themselves away in advance that even a despicable adversary can feign indulgence and step effortlessly aside.

Writing for yourself would be fine if you could ever really dismiss those who have composed your life's audience.

Drug habits could not encourage so much self-destruction without the collaboration of some remembered hostile voice that once convinced us defending ourselves was pointless.

'Free trade': trampling someone else's frail security for a 1% discount on your next gratuitous acquisition.

In his youth poverty was the fashion and he joined the communists; the day he inherited he switched to the conservatives. Both sides were fool enough to regard his treachery as something more intellectual than the barking of a dog for the pack and for food. They paid him to tell his meaningless story, paid others to attack it.

Weaklings need to rescue nonexistent damsels from nonexistent dragons.

Identifying someone with their aggression and anger is as unjust as identifying them with their bowels; but why are there so many people who soil the rug at parties?

Society has already had some revenge on a privacy invader forced by the secrets of his trade into unending precautions against unjust anthologizing.

How many people's professional studies are driven by the quest for fair advantage?

Churchgoing murderers regard atheists as failures in life.

It must be possible to devise a society where no one ever has to be told: no matter what anyone does you can never even begin to escape the dominance of X. Human nature says that once you are X the goal is achieved.

The older you get, the more savagely debt attacks the faculties you need to escape it.

Failure to pity someone betrayed by the hateful rogues he is even now conspiring with to destroy us.

The desire for justice is nostalgia for moments when it still seemed possible to defend ourselves against those who harmed us. The hope of mankind lies in someone whose nostalgia goes to the core of the damage.

In the uniform of a despised enemy you feel cheapened.

Given the energy-intensiveness of livestock, what better emergency measure against the destruction of the planet's farmland than a revival of the traditional Persian insistence that anyone guilty of slaughtering a harmless beast shall remain a pariah no matter how many miracles he performs? Doubly salutary, since it did not apply to noxious animals: hawks' heads would be cut off for their evil deeds; our elections would never be the same.

In a higher-dimensional space our banalities are never more than a millimeter away from the most piquant discoveries. The most petit of bourgeois is only an inch away from Wilde, through a diamond wall.

Fortune grants certain successes only on condition of breaking our heart.

Sin sees reluctance to ruin others as cowardice.

The quest for neurotic glory can yield fruits as spectacular as the alchemical search for the Philosopher's Stone; but a neurotically vindictive majority triggers the paradox of democracy.

She despised the passivity she thought she perceived in his sudden noncommittal stance, so she proceeded to justify it by replacing him.

The cruelest thing about spurious aggression is its blissful unconsciousness of its idiotic motives. Nature herself has entitled them to be self-deceivers.

Just when we convince ourselves our defenses are all Maginot Lines some atavistic enemy declares real war across the frontier we had once protected so well. If we had gone on wasting our time and money he would have let us bleed ourselves, then attacked Nice.

Someone who affects to despise the Underground Man is denying the theory of evolution. Either the higher faculties exist on a more primitive superstructure or they do not. It was the Underground Man who was part of a great artist's soul, not his well-adjusted comrades.

Her smile was so hackneyed that her eyes no longer bothered to go along for the ride.

At an unsuccessful dinner party what should be a product with many terms reduces itself to a simple expression.

Nietzsche's flirtations with aggressive amorality may have been nothing more than attempts at an ersatz for the necessary modicum of self-confidence others supply with *Lebenslügen.* Say you are in a world of neurotics animated by private, insanely vague dreams of glory. You construct an artificial neurosis in the hope of activating the vigorous hormones without yourself regressing to a thinly veiled baboon. In the real number system the highest values have devalued themselves, so you invent complex numbers and quaternions. You posit a thought-construct called N for Napolean. The actual expression for this construct might be $N + 7i + 6j$. A blockhead sees only the N and complains that the construct failed to conquer Europe, while he has successfully trashed a South Asian city at the touch of someone else's button. His model is real, yours is childishly inaccurate; moreover you are neurotic while he is an humanitarian. You demonstrate this by going mad in the street while he is counting his retirement money.

Each new generation of psychiatric drugs claims it has finally provided the clear, sober equanimity promised by the Hindus.

Once you grasp people's absolute contempt for one another your freedom from the desire for anyone's approbation can make you more vulnerable to their malice.

Aging must be in part the cellular stress of an ever-increasing mound of possible blackmails.

Even if we have the courage to risk our lives on a project we may cringe at the taunts about throwing life away.

When the warmonger meme causes pneumonia it thinks it has proven the inferiority of the untainted organism.

Why would mediocrity perfected not sneer at genius gone astray?

The longer it takes someone to grasp an implication of an idea the more likely he is to lord its success over those who long ago gave up on it in disgust with the learning curve of the market.

If you lined up all the people whose major achievement was senseless infringement upon others it would reach to Alpha Centauri and back.

Reducing people to their vices is fair play only in proportion to their worldly power; reflexive contradiction is honest only for privately jump-starting a weak battery.

What a blissful day when a woman's wicked intrigue turns out to have been motivated by love after all!

Overshoot the mark you are aiming at but do not aim above 45 degrees.

A permanent giddiness seems to take hold of certain people upon the discovery that there is no God to penalize them for giving their money upon usury and taking reward against the innocent. They must imagine themselves breaking through to the vital secret of Genghis.

Depression is consistent contemptus mundi. Today's brain chemistry as yesterday's religious ideal.

The dollarizing worldview says economic and verbal murder is an improvement on physical murder. Only the dead could decide this.

Finishing an indeterminate project under deadline is like saying goodbye at the intercontinental air terminal: the person you are kissing is not really still there.

Youth scoffs at the mockery of the internal curmudgeon reminding it of the complications bound to ensue from a wish. It is only a wish, and besides, we have so much vigor that if we are wounded we may not even notice it before the perpetrator is out of reach.

The sense of futility, a glitch in the fuel injectors. You accept an invitation, wondering whether you will still be alive on the night. You compromise yourself on the assumption that further damage to your reputation will not matter.

Judging by the suffering of the world, belief in a personal God is not error or trickery but wickedness.

Hilbert's basis theorem is a kind of answer to those who jest at the self-importance of human drops in the universal ocean. If that ocean should turn out to be something like an infinite series of integral expressions, it might have something like a basis set, on the human scale, with all the coefficients of the grand vistas merely intricate combinations of functions of the same variables. Not that we would really be able to figure out any of the invariants, but pretending otherwise would at least help the economy.

An inferior superior, a Procrustean bed.

The libels of corrupt ministers would reveal the entire disease of their hearts if we could only focus long enough.

The style that optimizes our mix of friends and enemies during our lifetimes spoils our rapport with future readers.

Watch the word 'democracy' tossed around casually despite insuperable class inequality and eventually you will cease to believe there is any difference at all between man and animal.

The more perfect market of today is dominated by capital gained in the less perfect market of yesterday.

Either all reason is divination or the world is small.

A type of human being that has grasped free speech only as the right to drown truth in money.

The crime of surveillance is to usurp the victim's prerogative of self-presentation. The first step in sentencing is permanent loss of self-presentation rights by globally accessible camera, but for some people this would be a reward rather than a punishment.

Fall in love and you find justice and virtue everywhere; fall in hate and you find injustice and vice; neither true love nor true hate is entirely mythical.

Political arsonists specialize in overheating your defense systems.

Ovid's remedies for love end in contempt for one person, but the yogic remedies for hate end in contempt for the whole spectacle of existence.

Only poetic and artistic personality equations should lack real roots. MIlitary surrealism bankrupts the State.

It is the absurdity of fortune that allows belief to conquer impossibility. The Newtonian rationality world history sometimes displays on the grand scale vanishes in the quantum realm of personalities, where stubborn follies find solvent mates.

Some habits seem deeply entrenched only because we have not yet stumbled across their surface mooring.

In praising businessmen for extracting greener money from each lump of metal, are we playing the Buddha tempting the children with greater rewards, or are we just sucking up to the ephemeral rich?

In the war on reality his id sent his ego out to negotiate on false premises. It represented them with so much ardor that instead of compromising on the true pleasure it got the full neurotic payoff.

Fidelity was rare, technical virtuosity rarer, love possibly nonexistent. To find them all at once you multiplied the probabilities and got an infinitesimal. So she preferred to train her lovers from scratch.

Lawyers running for office claim relying on precedent is the best training for the unprecedented.

The ego takes credit for things completely beyond its control, like the muscular capital required for bodybuilding.

He could mistreat all the workers because fantasies of promotion had a stronger hold on them than fear of dismissal. He could mistreat all the women because all they saw was how lavishly he supported the one. He thought it was he who had invented such optical illusions.

We would sleep more soundly some nights if the Procrustean bed of malice would simply chop off our heads.

False premises are so often vindicated by the event, or by the sheer number of fools, that it is never fully rational to admit even a stunning defeat. This principle lets opportunists advance themselves as far as they damage science.

Insult one mass man and you insult them all. You can hope they will be too dull to notice or you can be strong enough not to care.

Often a seeming reductio ad absurdum is just a legal but inappropriate substitution yielding $-1 = 5+8+11+...$ Occasionally the absurdity points to an arithmetic truth about something unfamiliar, a distance on some new curve.

Conservatism is the strong desire to minimize rational scrutiny of market imperfection.

Every law is a souvenir of an injustice, but some mementos are more nostalgic than others.

The moral numbing encouraged by television would be a yogic virtue if it turned the self into just another show.

Truthful libels bomb civilians too.

Excessive empathy tempts us to share even the indifference shallow people feel towards sound causes irrelevant to their incomes.

Social life is forever giving the lie to the assumption that it is intelligence which fits one for accurate anticipation of events. Knowing when to be a dullard is half of experience.

Newcomers from outside rally the discontented.

You are jaded when you have hardened yourself against ingratitude by privately regarding all loans as write-offs.

Our friends sometimes mistakenly praise our novelty or ingenuity at moments where we cannot correct them without embarrassing them. When they realize the truth they feel foolish if they do not start acting more skeptical even in cases where praise would be fair and badly needed.

You are suddenly confronted with the demand you take sides in an irrational quarrel.

He had not deserted her, merely given up hope of ever justifying her investment; she had not got him as far out of trouble as her vanity had led her to believe; the imaginary trap was too embarrassing for comment; straitjacketed gestures seemed more shameful than silence.

We hate fortune when she tricks us into defending ourselves with excessive force. Our opponent was using every weapon at his disposal, but he wanted us to think his attack was just an opening volley; by obliging his vanity we became his killers.

There are twelve sides to every quarrel.

Rats do not value yogic departure from the rat race.

Increasing our power means increasing the number of conflicting wills we must reconcile. Powerful friends mean contradictory claims for preeminence. Absolute power requires insensitivity to the insoluble.

Every common denominator in society demands a combination of talents as close at hand and as far away as a winning lottery combination.

Character assassination loves to masquerade as therapy. Spite and egotism love to masquerade as the hidden hand of progress.

We had the tool to avoid the mistake, but the toolbox was in disarray. Or: we stumbled across the hammer just as the nail walked in the door.

If possible let people bind themselves to you by what they give you rather than what you give them.

Mass communications augment fame and envy alike, and the net gain is doubtful.

A perfect parent could make art of most everything censorship would block.

Admiring great men means admiring fraud and force on a grand scale.

Cybernetic weaponry is the most impressive wimpus in history.

A gift to an ambitious man is like a single syringe to a heroin habitué.

Suitors tout their superior devotion as if acts were the source of affection.

The media offer the mind what a whore offers the body.

The yogi claimed not paranormal powers but supranormal: virtue.

Idiot-proof devices and situations are not necessarily intelligence-proof.

Obscure prose has become an endangered species. It deserves some environmental protection because the muddles it harbors are also chances for unusual projection. This is true even of unphilosophic bureaucrats: a general lying about murder in Latinisms Shakespeare would have parodied four hundred years ago can spill enough of the collective id accidentally to trigger a new sociology.

How can economic ends be viewed objectively by anyone whose desires are not sated? How can economic means be viewed objectively by anyone whose desires are?

A bored enemy sometimes forgives just for variety.

He recommended she get to know the dolphins better by spending a few weeks underwater, breathing through her gills.

A perquisite of high office is the chance for defamation so grave the victim never even learns of the charges.

Distrust of fractional reserve banking has something in common with skepticism about the existence of complex numbers.

She pretended to be a little hill, to watch the middling mountain feeling awesome.

Having no one to admire can be as corrosive as having no one to love.

We hypocritically insist that our suffering deserves to be more than a motion in the other person's optic nerve.

Attention is an addictive drug.

They thought the rich man might be more impressed with a gift representing a higher proportion of their negative net worth.

Vice laws insist that type X receive a type Y blood transfusion.

Retirement with great minds of the past allows us to die with their unsolved problems as well as our own.

The time required to catch up with the world is never as long or as short as the time spent in exile.

An honest hypocrite, eager to confess and make amends but certain the confession would cause more pain than the amends could remove.

If philosophy remains relatively barren it may only be for lack of a graphic notation such as a mechanical vocabulary of dream images. Before the invention of the calculus mathematics could not hope to cope with accurate description of organ pipes. Someone might have said it would never really pass beyond Mesopotamian gimmicks.

Women are closer than men to forgetting at will.

A writer with too obvious a trademark style has discovered the literary analogue of the theorem that any number can be expressed as the sum of three triangular numbers or four squares.

Evasion of entropy betokens a cellular intelligence that passes for cerebral.

A priest hardened to murder is pitiable in the same way as a rake. Both belabor the point about the arbitrariness of identity.

Once he would have been a eunuch astrologer in the golden musk-scented pavilion of the harem, but today he was John Q. Smith Memorial Scholar at the Defense Institute, analyzing the wimpus gap.

His ambitions ran to exhausted genres.

No one really believes in anyone else's free will.

Safest to assume injuries will be remembered forever and gifts forgotten immediately: gifts are finite, desire infinite.

Criticism rarely reforms either ourselves or others.

Do scribblers hurt the earth more when they cut down trees or when they build scribbling machines?

A majority must be huge before its fickle gratitude can offset the unswerving hatred of an injured minority.

Even two creatures identical in every molecule would not fail to reproach one another with deviation from perfection.

A thinker who raped truth, saying she wanted it.

Feign vulnerability where you are strongest or the enemy weakest.

The first time you realize you have handed the body more than it can recover from.

If people really remembered previous incarnations they would find nothing to dread in either suffering or death.

There are maddening allies who constantly compromise 49 percent of you. Every time you add even 2 percent of your own blundering you are freshly vulnerable to charges of being less than half credible. You marvel at the number of politicians who can endure this thin margin year after year.

The journalistic world regarded it as a great miracle that exponential growth in machine power could produce growth in wealth without an ever-growing labor pool flexing nonexistent muscle to increase wages.

Denying the importance of luck is the same as claiming you have both infinite knowledge and infinite ability to act upon it, i.e. that you are God.

Our vanity claims responsibility for the congruence between our abilities and others' desires.

Authors who churn out a book a year on questions of ultimate concern make you wonder why the universe decided to provide them so much more material.

Men are so insensitive that awareness of someone else's mood sometimes counts as telepathy even if the detailed contents of his mind are as opaque as ever.

The love of power as an end in itself is the desire to spend time with people we despise.

Solving her heat equation was a simple matter of transforming her comments to ellipsoidal coordinates.

Sometimes a daemonic miser stands guard over the treasure chest of memory to refuse us even the penny we need. Sometimes there is so much gold that it jams the hinges shut.

How could the need to fill precisely the same number of column inches every day not lead to distortion of relative importances?

We are no more entitled to our biological than our financial inheritance.

Rascals have a superior feel for the remarkable staying power of a determined lie.

Astonishment at the profligacy of heirs is like astonishment that a passenger is not a pilot.

Harshness and cruelty to straw men makes us fairer to the real ones.

The perfect worldling could never be threatened without remembering that everyone tries to exaggerate his authority.

Where values contradict one another everyone must have some taint on his reputation.

Encourage factions to debate until hatred yields to boredom.

By simple abuse of courtesy they could waste enormous time and energy in petty conflict. These Lilliputian ropes, as malicious and callow as a girls' school plot, seemed to them a wonderfully clever strategy; whenever he broke them they could denounce him as a savage brute, and whenever they irritated him like flies swarming around a horse he was sure to make some mistake with his few remaining friends.

Salespeople do for some women what hustlers do for men.

You can almost always afford to beat a competitor by 1 percent.

Better to be stingy by choice than necessity.

People who rely on state secrecy are bombing others from a safe distance.

The success of journalism is our perpetual surprise at the petty personal motives behind quarrels over principle.

Rarely is it entirely clear why other people are so worried about their secrets.

Everyone is born with a modicum of foolish trust. Not something you want to save for a rainy day.

You have not seen all of life until your hopes have slowly drowned in compound interest.

One pessimism believes the imagination contradicts reality; another, that it contradicts itself.

Love of possessions is love of the hormones their contemplation secretes.

The atheist's tragedy is that sin can quite happily send you off to hell right here in Paradise even if there is no God. All you need is for someone to install a permanent contradiction between your self-image and your self. Fire and brimstone are nothing by comparison with the torments of a conscience discovering its own existence at the wrong moment.

Paranoid misanthropy said: never forego a dishonest satisfaction for the sake of someone who has secretly betrayed you.

Even if you are strong enough to despise revenge you must sometimes play at it to avoid the appearance of weakness.

Given enough education you can hold yourself and your friends up to constant unbearable scrutiny.

He thought it was for her sake he was refraining from suicide.

Plant accurate predictions about yourself in your audience to make them feel clever when they come true.

When your resources dry up you must procrastinate in the hope of rescue.

Everyone has something to say, just as there is a finite continued fraction for every rational number.

The invisible handcuffs made her seem wasteful of opportunity.

When a politician violates the law of nations we want to say, well, yes, obviously if you just break the law...

Discretion requires a secrecy that ends up saturating pleasure with anxiety.

The consolation prize was to be conscious of the beginning of the end.

When affluence blunts the cruelty of your competitors the booby prize can have the highest net value. There is a great surplus, and everyone is so happy to feel superior.

Skepticism is paint remover that eventually blisters the user's hands.

The same instinct that makes people expect to win a lottery makes them think you own the combined favors of all the people who appear to be your friends.

A failure who could perfectly anticipate the outcome of any bet he had not actually placed.

Never talk about anything that you do not know to be to your advantage.

A perfect education would cloud each child's life with slander for a full year, to prepare him for this world where even Zarathustra was framed by envious competitors.

Prudent and prodigal lives are both rewarded by death.

Did Freud know he was elaborating on the Charvak sect of Hindu skeptics, who said plainly that Brahma, Vishnu and Mahadeo were just representations of the sex organs and that religious practitioners were unwittingly just trying to outdo cows, owls, bears and snakes at their own silly games?

Perhaps we are simultaneously or orthogonally lived in other temporal directions by people who assemble from worms or ashes and grow ever more youthful and hopeful until they enter Nirvana and are sucked up into others.

Habitual discounting of the world's habitual lies saps the energy it appears to save.

Fate sometimes attacks us the same way a conspiracy might, but without offering any personalities we could use as a handle to fight back; an invisible enemy is a hundred possible enemies.

Poverty lets you enjoy some of the benefits of senility in a youthful body. Pleasures take on the same unreality they must have at ninety.

Worldly wisdom is the final refinement of paranoia, dissembling its global war with the collective id.

Frigidity is infidelity between jobs.

He spent a lifetime attacking sophists he had only seen long enough for them to defame him.

The equation of a person is one degree higher than their dimensionality.

The demiurge has a weakness for cheap irony and paradox.

Many religions aim to freeze moods. Not much could distress us were we able to chop life into an infinite series of still frames; but freezing conscious moods usually means starting unconscious tempests.

Cruel fortunes accredit their victims as doctors of failure and apathy.

Even superb education cannot fully replace the natural inability to distinguish between well-calculated risk and herd warmth.

Give a bully the impression that winning you over is not quite impossible and will reflect well on him.

Man is the slandering animal.

Several layers of secret thoughts: the first to simulate frankness and intimacy; the second to inspire fear of unconscious brilliance; the third to renounce the world.

The habit of contradicting ordinary lies will eventually stumble into refuting a life-lie.

Earth would be fair, they said, and all men glad and wise, if only they were given real guns to destroy the phantoms their bigotry projected. Only they were courageous, they said, because only they faced up to the grave dangers they hallucinated and fabricated. Only they were honest enough to condemn the imaginary daemon as it deserved. Only they had the stomach for the risk of national bankruptcy which had to be taken if they and their cronies were to receive capital proportionate to their moral grandeur. Only they understood the concept of freedom well enough to force it upon others at gunpoint. Only they really grasped what violent loathing they deserved, and consequently how much violence would be necessary to obstruct what the foolish goyim called justice; the terrifying blindness of everyone else was a national emergency.

To recover from a reputation for deceit you must marshal truths irresistible to your listeners' hope and vanity.

Mobs believe that if you do not mouth platitudes you do not grasp them.

He imagined that if he just kept on smashing away at every foundation in sight, sooner or later he was bound to come up with something as fruitful as non-Euclidean geometry.

When in doubt, assume your opponent infinitely vain.

In the military-industrial State voters pay for the privilege of being forbidden rational choice.

Religions say all tigers are paper.

Odd how the heroism of laissez-faire capitalism fares so well in a political environment where the feminine majority has supposedly outgrown Prince Charming.

Fortune will be happy to give you anything you have honestly outgrown.

Success against a traitor means planting false secrets whose betrayal will make him not only a slanderer but a credulous fool.

Every use of ignoble means strengthens their presence in the world.

Wherever you are about to present indisputable proof of your virtue, make sure to foster the cruelest possible doubts about yourself beforehand and to feign unconsciousness of your vindication.

It takes many years to realize instinctively how much net profit we reap every time we make someone feel intellectually superior.

Sin is other people's mistakes.

Perfectionist enough to waste part of the opportunity.

Many people do not need Cicero or Hume to hold miracles in contempt, and falsely conclude that they do not need Cicero or Hume for anything.

Overly difficult problems are no more use than overly difficult weights. Growth means working to failure, not demanding failure.

People who believe in astrology are acting out Descartes' dubious dictum that you should start walking in some direction rather than none.

The job of governments is to convince you the best things in life are the ones presently offered for sale.

Trying to kill extravagant supernatural claims with science is like trying to put out a fire with a polygon. You need fascist edicts such as "Congress shall make no law concerning an establishment of religion".

The main purpose of news is to convey misleading trends.

In every misfortune short of natural catastrophe the most indigestible thing is realizing how our unconscious let us down.

Do not assume your opponent will suddenly change his habits in favor of reason or virtue.

Punishing people whose inclinations are different from ours is a good way to cheat them out of economic opportunity.

When the market for our talents vanishes we risk forgetting they still exist. After being bludgeoned with foreign successes for months we stumble across something more lasting, left propped in an odd part of our psyche in some rushed moment, covered with dust but still mechanically sound, and it is hard to remember who hypnotized us into sleepwalking away from it.

Incorrigibly aggressive people live in a world of things rather than persons.

Conceal your dislike of someone as long as you safely can.

There are as many forms of human interaction as there are ways to multiply hyper-numbers.

Even with the best maxims the user's manual is missing.

Sometime in his life a skilled negotiator will extract something he does not need from someone who needs it desperately.

She overlooked her transition from discontent to desperation.

Sophists think it cleverer to let someone else pay the price of confronting ubiquitous error. If your model is better, how is it they have all the money?

A politician whose greatest distinction was to have killed the truth in matters of supreme concern.

Corruption approaches perfect indifference to the merit of the scapegoat.

Ignobility regards successful abuse of courtesy as proof of superior cunning.

Part of us agrees that the gospel of meekness and renunciation is a fraud peddled by the ambitious. Yet their denial of commonality with their victims betrays an intellectual inferiority we would be ashamed to share.

If political candidates were required to campaign in the nude parliaments would consist of 20-year-old women and 30-year-old men.

Worship of success is usually worship of blood money.

Who is better equipped to project the price of the average conscience, a hero or a scoundrel?

Educational costs are society's confession that it regards truth primarily as an assault weapon: pay at the handle or you will pay at the blade. Someone who makes a million shuffling titles to land is said to have justified the investment of a hundred thousand in a literary education.

Patent law says Bruno at the stake and Galois in his cell did it for the money. It says that what ended up being done for two bags of gold would never have been done for the hope of only one. Formerly an inventor needed months just to set up an overseas office; now he can pack a billion sales presentations into a single day. Hence the government insists patent terms must be lengthened.

Electoral democracy says mediocrity is an end rather than a means.

Sporus once said that a poor man refusing to choose between two falsely reformed crooks must be too happy to care about trivialities like politics.

What use is a lie whose beauty is too subtle to make fools reach for their wallets?

Iago is the spirit of experimentation run amok.

Lack of interest is not an achievement.

The voluptuous sensation of plausibility ended in the chancres of mental syphilis.

Revulsion can far outlive the desire for revenge, keeping the smug malice of our enemies alive long after we thought we had digested their injustices and recovered the ability at least to feign indifference.

When events conspire they might as well be persons.

Everyone wants a discount on everyone else's personality. This makes some people position themselves as wholesale to the public, others as not for sale.

The future is so uncertain that any firm statement about it can fuel the imagination.

If you cannot articulate the secret of your success, is it really you that had it?

Quarrels are exercises with weights; ruptures are pulled muscles.

Every cross-section of the universe is an organism desiring and suffering. The random collection of objects on a dirty desk considers itself a martyr when it is finally cleaned up.

How could misunderstanding not prevail in a world where the daily actions of any four people can fill an encyclopedia?

The decisive point had seemed too obvious to mention and was now impossible to reconstruct.

We are falsely surprised when someone who has done wonders in an ellipsoid space collapses in a spherical or Euclidean.

Surveillance revealed terrible distress, a delicate situation one would not willingly have disturbed.

People like experienced help: they want any upcoming deprivations to be experienced by those who already know weakness.

An enemy who knows just what sort of thorn would suit your rose.

The fifteenth-century Sikh sage Bábá Nânac, who thoughtfully escorted the damned from at least one of the hells upon his demise, wore the Musselman rosary in one hand and the Hindu Zunar religious thread as a necklace. He thought that to the extent that you damaged any of God's creatures you could fairly be regarded as insincere in your devotion to God. What wonderful progress we have made in theology since this barbaric Kashmiri. We no longer require atavistic notions of religious pluralism; any lie or murder whatsoever is enough to sanctify us as the only thing that matters, what Sanskrit calls Yid, cosmically false consciousness.

Why did people resent his helping them to be something superior to what they were?

No one will ever really be able to teach anyone else when an enterprise is premature or overripe. It will always be a comedy.

Righteous adherence to a cause is something enemies usually share.

In the beginning love has clear integrals and differentials everywhere. One day you find something continuous but not differentiable or with random sums. If your luck fails it is all petty anomalies and infinitely dusty examinations of the fundamental laws of arithmetic; you have to content yourself pondering cuts in the number line, or odd mappings, when before you got a juicy series.

Assume no one will ever forgive any injury; never assume someone you offended has interests greater than harming you.

Appeal to an authority your audience is too stupid to understand but not ignorant enough to be unaware of.

Excessive detail can obscure our vision, so some prefer to know nothing at all before passing judgment.

As soon as you make a choice the risks you have accepted become real while those you rejected become unreal. Part of you feels foolish for choosing real over unreal dangers.

Many of the accusers we do not get to confront are in other people's unconscious minds.

Introspection is so weak that projection can be the only hope of seeing our faults.

Christ lacked or despised the self-confidence to manipulate Pilate at the crucial, easy moment. He must have known this worldly man would have been amused to find him aware the mob accusations were gibberish. Instead Christ said Thou Sayest, ie. "whatever".

Some characters need the phases of their lives to be coitus interruptus.

Real acceptance of mortality mocks the pretensions of health crusaders pretending one infinitesimal is bigger than another.

Desperate adversaries are hardest to war game.

The first shall be last. Respect for X makes us ashamed to confide in him, so the person who deserves the most honesty gets the least.

Ignorant malice breaks rules of engagement a worthy enemy would at least know.

A remark suppressed from fear of betraying personal bitterness may be the most objective thing we have ever said

Surveillance seeks pornography and finds gynecology.

To harden the soul against chronic danger courage may be forced to empty the psychic treasury.

Age is wiser because disease dispels the illusion of seamless connection with reality.

Technocrats wish to pretend only other people have prehistoric brain layers.

Wilde in his cell tries vainly to convince himself it was a hidden fate rather than a stupid ape that forced him into the arms of Christ.

Some travel to fill an empty mind, others to clean out the attic.

Less bitter to be outdone by an honest rascal than a childish hypocrite.

Wickedness hiding from itself in neurotic fantasies of moral rectitude outrages once by its aggression and twice by its immaturity.

Humility is wisdom because nearly all attempts to overcome our inbred mutual contempt are futile.

Beneath her worn and soiled covers he found an exquisite translation of a Persian classic, without a single page cut by the multitude of scholars who claimed to have passed her way.

Cowardice in defeat is less reprehensible than hubris in victory; courage in defeat and egotism in victory are animal virtues.

Advising someone to address the unconscious roots of their conflicts rather than the superficial conscious symptoms means shipping them off to access the inaccessible.

She radiated good-natured contempt on the worthy and unworthy alike.

Too late we discover how little was necessary to save our friends and ourselves.

Hypocrisy likes to see itself as multidimensionality.

Discreet brown-nosing regards its success as proof of subtle rectitude.

False maturity laughs at the abstraction of justice, and false virtue feigns outrage at the cheap cynicism of those who hate its cheap cynicism.

Many truths are entirely self-evident and constantly forgotten, such as that market value is not an intrinsic quality of objects or people.

What makes the tyranny of a twentieth-century majority any less base than the tyranny of an eighteenth-century monarch?

With empathy as with theology, a little experience leads you to despise it and more experience leads you to despise the despisers.

A prince who commits murder has the option of blaming it on an adviser, or taking pride in the relative infrequency of his murders.

You are lucky when the person who has earned your hatred imagines himself too lofty to care about your opinion.

If you do not pose as a loser you will never discover who loves you for yourself; every animal loves a winner.

"Natural and organic" products are the Versailles pastoral of our bourgeoisie.

Putting down some rebellions gratifies vanity as little as cleaning up after dog vomit.

If major profits come before the market is aware competition is worthwhile, what do major profits have to do with capitalism?

A perfect rake is a male lipstick lesbian.

Always war game massive retaliation.

The confessional is a confession that confiding in a friend is usually confiding in the world.

Feign fear of losing something and you will see who takes pleasure in stealing it.

Classical satire exaggerates the ability of women to misrepresent their affections.

When fortune grows bored she thumbs through the less likely outcomes.

Dada obsolete: instead of stifling the anti-reality drive with psychoanalysis, one now pampers it with an arsenal and a cabinet post.

Hypocrisy may declare bankruptcy when you least expect it.

The house may usually win; still, a coin tossed an infinite number of times will contain gargantuan stretches of any pattern that might suit you.

Political centrism is the systematic confusion of moderation and mediocrity.

Force pollutes its object by staining it with our will.

Decide as if you would live forever and execute as if you would die tomorrow.

Vice laws that prohibit mental states regardless of criminal consequences assert ownership of souls.

Collective neurosis is the stock-in-trade of political consultants.

Anyone who can consistently count his blessings has extra eyes in the back of his head.

He forgave her because it amused him to see forgiveness might really exist.

Demagogues tell mobs the devil is only in the details.

If you make only one demand at a time you will have only one group of opponents at a time.

Many maxims simply by stating a dichotomy give a false impression of telling you which side to come down on when.

Appeal to the ignorance of bystanders.

We project illusory coherence onto others' reference frames like crows building a scarecrow.

By masking out a certain function of her conversation he could make it diatonic.

Telling someone you need them is telling them to be an ego.

A philosopher king would have the strength to discard the noble lie.

Secrecy in revenge is a sign of vulnerability in the weak and pusillanimity in the strong.

Fraudulent liberties are the best-gilt political chains.

In a curved space where vectors move along geodesics a person may appear to be flailing wildly when really he is whizzing along the line of least resistance.

Vulgarity thinks majorities are ends in themselves.

Byron's bluestockings with their "science and lobster salad" now control their own regiments.

Capital feels the value of its old money is the value of its new time.

You rarely go wrong assuming another person regards you as raw material.

Every success is a pyramid scheme.

Medical progress vindicates supposedly half-baked genes.

Alienation and deprivation lend society the appearance of a bees' nest.

A coupon-clipping philosopher assures us suicide is no general solution to the self-alienation of the World Spirit.

Finally the burn victim got a glass of water.

You are supposed to know enough precedents to avoid false claims of originality. You are supposed to know few enough precedents to make false claims of originality.

Legal fees are commissions on someone's obfuscation.

Perfect irresolution signals suicide, a poisoned will ripe for random invasion.

Journalism is an addictive drug offering all the poisons specified by Patanjali: injury, untruth, theft, incontinence, avarice, uncleanliness, discontent, lack of endurance, talkativeness, thinking of the character of low persons or of ungodly attributes. With other drugs you merely share needles; with this one you share the substance too, and need philosophical methadone to give it up.

The player could not face the audience that night and did not want to choose another role.

Which is more valuable, doing your duty or avoiding animosities?

"Terrorist" is a medieval Yiddish theological term meaning "my outraged victim".

If you change your mind when it is too late to stop the train, conceal it so you will at least appear consistent if your original plan turns out right.

When your enemies quarrel, leave them alone to kill each other unless you are certain their mutual enmity is greater than their hatred of you.

Why does a female hermit seem more unusual than a male?

Envy is a form of radioactivity: a small dose is not much less lethal than a moderate one. If you must do the time, do the crime.

Public favors have to be divided amongst a million people so it is hardly surprising they will inspire less gratitude than personal favors.

Commuting between the frying pan and the fire.

Knowing that all crowd passions are vulgarities is not always enough to show you where the fallacy lies.

What would stupid, wicked men want with intelligent virtue? Most everyone asks themselves this about most everyone else.

The magic of compound interest: young women traditionally receive the prize for vanity, but who is more vain than someone who keeps jacking up his hourly rate long after his death?

Sententiousness is a venereal risk of philosophy.

Spacial relativity applies in the moral world too, when we find we have been watching the heights from the valley instead of vice-versa.

Cigarette smoking: black pranyayama.

Hereditary power can coast where new power has to innovate. It does not have to levy new military taxes because there is no revolution to consolidate, no fresh enemies sapping the resources that maintain friendships. Religious power can coast even more.

The new boss had better legs than the old boss, so much the worse.

If you were watching a play and the characters started shooting real bullets at the audience you would call it a bad play. Optimism disagrees.

Kill the entire family of your competitor.

Innovators have the status quo for enemies and speculators for friends.

After too many years you realize the full implications of an injustice you thought you had survived; you see your shabby enemy glorying in the fruits of crime, his stunted conscience plump with complacent inauthenticity.

Nonviolent revolution requires a tired tyrant.

Hell is the impossibility of grace.

Luck throws you a roof and expects you to build the walls and foundation.

Proper sex education covers preemptive nuclear strike in the war between the sexes.

Ruling is for people who do not mind being preoccupied with war.

Only longstanding death can wipe away the stain of genius' estrangement from the banal motivations of market-makers.

Practiced evil has a headstart on anyone even tempted to virtue.

You know your self-confidence is gone when the voice in your head starts sounding like someone you loved so long ago you can no longer remember what your street address was then. They might for all you know have improved greatly in the interim but they are a stranger again, their word subject to compounding discounts. You remind yourself that there is no one but you left to take care of this orphan, who after all once loved you without question and did you so many favors. But you are no longer able to trust. It might have gone desperado, ripping you off for a quick commission.

If you are likely to lose anyway, the odds in favor of prudence evaporate.

Squandering other people's things is good for your reputation, squandering your own kills it.

People would rather offend someone they love than someone they fear.

The deceiver always finds a fresh gull.

Walk down the street and watch those who have hit zero. That is you, with all your property, all your friendly clients, all your income, your dignity, your food snatched by some victorious mediocrity. In a shop window some broadcast rogue argues all will be well for those who clean his toilet at minimum wage.

Everyone is vulgar enough to worship what benefits them over what damages them; only the masochist is refined enough to ignore the difference.

An economist who advocated low-rate loans to the poor found his ideas usurped a generation later by cunning politicians taking commissions from humanitarian usurers.

The majesty of the state is a gown worn by just and unjust alike.

Secretly provoke a fight with someone whom you can increase your renown by conquering.

I told a prosperous Talmudist that a rich Christian was a contradiction in terms and he looked at me as if the irony were my own childishness.

The Italian philosophers warn you all the time that each party has reason to distrust a neutral. But how much has neutrality hurt the Swiss?

An overly powerful ally becomes your boss after the war.

Market clearing is a unicorn because arbitrage rewards concealment.

All praise is flattery.

Make sure telling you the plain truth is seen as great daring and lying to you a hanging offense.

Algorithmic art is the final vindication of Plato over Aristotle. You will be able to make love with a mathematical formula which age cannot wither nor custom stale; you will become one.

We notice the thoughts of great men in our everyday lives much the same way birds notice the concept of number but discard it as an idle curiosity.

If there were limits to the dishonesty of the majority one could condition oneself simply to fall silent at the first sensation of outrage; injustice would expose itself promptly enough; but life is so short.

The devil is happiest when our best qualities are the cause of our downfall. Because we were away promptly attending to our duties, we were missing at the moment our presence could have prevented a disastrous mistake.

Manners are the spelling and syntax of morals; their history is linguistic history, a catalog of errors ratified by people who might have known better.

The world is the perpetual calculation of an irrational number to infinite decimal places, and its absurdity is the endlessly diminishing return on enhanced precision. Like pi, its simplicity is happy to yield endless stretches of digits meeting our oversubtle tests for randomness or for concealed algebraic series, or cabalistic messages. Religious simplicity insists these stretches are part of the ratio between a radius and a circumference.

Necessity is sometimes merely the great-aunt of invention, providing solutions too long after the problem has done its evil.

Sexual cruelty kills the enthusiasm that excites it.

The mantra was said to have been revealed to J. Alsworth (later Lord Smythe) in 1767 by an itinerant native of Kashmir, the wandering Sufi sheikh Modan the Impermanent, at one point a courtier to a Persian prince and, before his banishment, author of the "Twilight Rose" series of ascetic devotional epics. We could not trace it back any further than a Detroit advertising agency, and had given it up as a hoax when we discovered that the ad man had stumbled across the genuine article when he followed a lady into a downtown mosque after a three-martini lunch. There, between a fast-food restaurant and a brothel, we found a seven-hundred-year-old manuscript arguing the physical reality of imaginary numbers as a tool in Allah's arsenal against the infidel.

Someone who really believes the journey is more important than the goal has never spent ten years walking to Limbo.

Even the least educated people are intrigued by the discovery of an ancient manuscript clearly anticipating modern discoveries: an oblique blow at the pretensions of modern technocrats.

The war of interests makes it prudent to encrypt our emotions; neurosis starts with the loss of the key.

Well begun is half frustrated.

Half our problems come from failure to generalize what we know perfectly well.

Spying is theft of intellectual property; entrapment trespasses at the fountain of motivation.

Leverage the victim's guilt. In the 'honey trap with bees', after your woman has seduced him and goaded him with blackmail, murder her with his knife.

You almost always get more from the sublimation than the gratification of an illicit desire.

Neurosis is confusion between logical impossibility and empirical difficulty.

To give someone's morale a little windfall, feign a mistake whose refutation was thought too commonplace for retail sale.

Plan on mercenaries leaving or assaulting you as soon as battle begins.

Satan wanted humanity to have a prime number of fingers and toes; God wanted four or six; they compromised at ten.

In English employment is called a 'job', after the Biblical character the devil was permitted to torment with impunity.

Male sine wave, female cosine.

Paltriness is the saving grace of many corruptions. Only an eccentric sneered when a usurper charged the public for the time and effort needed to squander a bag of its cash on finery for a conference on optimal capital allocation.

Usurpers want authority for the same reason monkeys want pearl necklaces.

Someone who has never been able to grasp the difference between intellectual life and a fashion show has the same advantage as the stockbroker with a dartboard.

Eventually the pendulum will swing back to serious doubt whether women should be allowed to take public oaths.

Courage as useless as the muscles of a weightlifter stranded in the Sahara.

A child who spent a single year reviewing every lie in the newspapers would have everything needed to succeed in economic life.

When someone we regarded as a moral agent turns out nothing but a bundle of desires, their success becomes the devaluation of everything education seeks to achieve, forcing us into the kind of bankruptcy inventors face before the masses have grasped the implications of their innovations.

Christian educators dare not press home the central image of the faith. To tell the children their best contributions will be stolen and their reputations blackened beyond repair by apelike scoundrels would discourage them beyond the ability to look after themselves.

As competition grows fiercer children will eventually have to become adults at the age of five, building real fortunes. Will they also learn to overcome the nihilist impasse at the age of seven?

A jackdaw made fun of a philosopher out of date enough to believe there was still such a thing as a proletariat.

Betrayal saddles us with phantom limbs.

When we die we will look in the great book of life and see all the forgotten innovators, all the friends whose nearby existence we never suspected, all the harm we inadvertently did, the opportunities missed to our advantage and disadvantage, the love and indifference masquerading behind anger and fawning, the secret ambitions and unconscious motives that resisted analysis to the end, the true parentage of children and paintings, the origins of canards, the successful blackmail, the unjust verdict, the moments when corruption and cancer irrevocably seized lives, the mathematical secrets beyond our grasp, the art of cultivating plants that think and speak, the expansion or eternal recurrence of the universes.

Pascal's wager remains ridiculous if only a sadistic God could place the clues of immortality so far out of our reach. We might as well bet that Satan will reward those with the courage to dismiss the frivolous illusion of empathy and boldly betray everyone in sight.

Compatibility meter: you are walking along the street when suddenly the device rubs your leg to say the unassuming person you just passed is the love of your life.

Constant surveillance collapses libido.

Most laws against perversion rest on the reasoning: if God had meant us to have electricity He would not have hidden coal underground.

Perfect mental balance is stasis.

The honorable Congressman explained that he came from one of the seven existential spheres below the belt of the Almighty, that to confine our representatives to the seven spheres above would reduce the colorful diversity of America, that his pedophilia was the perfect evolutionary spice to turbocharge the health and attractiveness of the country's young males.

How many books would still be written if their authors understood how they look to secondhand booksellers fifty years later?

Her grotesque egotism had always made her easy to reckon with, but now here she was asking him a sensitive question about himself. Had she somehow taken an interest in another person? Was she determined to unearth some potentially damaging souvenir before her return to self-absorption? No, fortunately she had merely given uncharitable credence to an idiotic rumor he could brush aside with his little finger; sixty seconds later she was admiring herself for being so understanding: who but she had experienced the range of jealous slurs required to teach such exquisite empathy with the plight of her maligned friends?

No one has really solved the problem of three point-mass bodies acting upon one another in empty space, yet no one is ashamed to vote on what to do about three billion minds acting upon one another in the atmosphere. Some are shameless enough to stand for office.

The dignity of other people's labor. The spur of poverty makes other people more productive. They are more autonomous when taking orders, more independent when dependent on marketplace whims, more religious when their material ambitions increase, more philosophical when they prefer symbolic rewards to no reward. They raise wages by flooding labor markets and acquire property by paying us interest. Their money is not as hard-earned because they do not understand risk as we do.

Surprisingly few words are designed to model reality.

Reports relishing someone's faults can generate the false conclusion that genuine virtue is under assault by envy and spite.

Politics pretends oppression is really correlativity.

If inheritance were made illegal, why would markets not intervene to substitute other motives?

The only people who have really understood Seneca's philosophy were on the other end of his usury. Compound interest for me, noble equanimity for you.

The context of our indispensability is dispensable.

Your first lottery ticket increases your odds infinitely, your second infinitesimally.

The moment when a memory ceases to move us is a death in our family.

Someone who left behind every trace of ignorance and temporal provincialism would become invisible.

One indiscretion can inoculate us against all the rest.

Alcoholics have given themselves over to a Higher Power long before they attempt reform.

Some must give to the State so that others may merely lend.

Overly sharp logic insists courage hold up under nuclear attack, or eroticism under klieg lights.

Salvation by works is impossible because good works create targets for evil.

Perfect renunciation includes renunciation of painful standards.

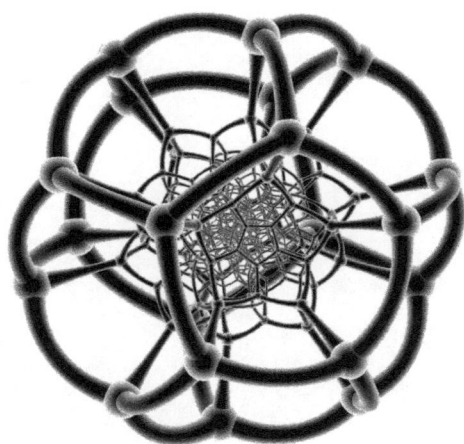

The progressive universal poetry of the authoritarian perverts. When you can cross wires at will you can use torture as food for laughter and orgasm.

She bragged about using masturbation to dispense with men, then vilified men who turn the tables. Yogic schism.

Rhinestones are proud they have fewer flaws than diamonds.

The man who admires the political power of the lie will also admire the biological power of the flu, the olfactory power of sewage.

Meditation performs judo on egotism by amplifying it into absurdity.

Fame. Nietzsche despised the Reich and traced the fiendish cunning of Jewish priests back to ancient Aryan corruption. Schopenhauer denied the existence of the white race. Both had their reputations tarred with Hitler's brush.

Restlessness, stupefaction, distraction are the unsolicited sales calls of the unconscious. Focus puts you on the solicitor's "do not call" list, withdrawal puts you on everyone's.

If you write "Am I dreaming?" on a little piece of paper in your wallet and pinch yourself every time you see it you will eventually find yourself reading it in a lucid dream. If you write "deceased, return to sender" on inflammatory correspondence from your unconscious you will eventually bore the devil enough to send him away for a good long holiday. But real focus is so rare that even people who have seen these magic tricks in action seldom manage to make them ineradicable habits. If you succeed, please make the check out to me.

Dead desires make very convincing zombies.

The theory of evolution and natural selection contains demons and goblins and witches, the brute creature layers left over in our bodies from earlier epochs; when they appear as our inner voice they often steal the guise of civilized men and women.

Sincere self-deception is black magic.

A train of thought as popular as chlamydia.

Attachment likes to show off its pretty needle marks.

You become a leader in environmental protection by tithing ten percent of the money you got razing the Amazon.

Psychological economics: repression, neurosis and vice persist where their expected net profit is higher than the expected net profit of reality.

Enlightenment is a limit process where the material differential approaches zero.

The moral world is a free lottery financing itself with negative jackpots.

He marveled at the stupidity of someone who would use logic where character assassination would do.

Are monkeys ever ashamed of imitating another monkeys?

If wisdom were about better models of 3-D reality there would not be so many stories of sages falling for the silliest cons, tripping down obvious wells. The man who always models his interests correctly knows the details of the world like a collector knows the three hundred thousand varieties of postal stamp; but wisdom says that the coordinate system of the world has very many more than three mutually perpendicular axes, that all its pretty 3-D ingenuities are as dimensionally desiccated as lines in a world of surfaces.

Asceticism rings false because God made the seven deadly sins; libertinism rings false because God made the hope of fidelity.

To save time she threw away the ladder while climbing it.

If science progresses far enough, malicious computer instructions designed to disable love robots will break the hearts of billions.

With the ancient Indians, every time you think you are talking to a disembodied god he turns into a child and vice-versa. One second he is going on about great oceans in the sky filled with sugar-water, wine, and milk; you roll your eyes; the next he has placed a universe three hundred billion light years long inside an egg which itself is nothing more than a firefly in the sky; how could all the cunning paradoxes of set theory produce any better intuition of infinities?

Bovine placidity sees human life as something that grows in your stomach.

Most of the time morality says not to do but to be something different. A great many moral injunctions make no sense unless they are presumed addressed to yogis in perfect control of specific hormones.

"You can do X, because A did X". Only a neurological genius could be entirely certain.

Faulting philosophers for technological naivete is not unlike faulting a biologist for not being a chemist.

Insipid subtleties for the initiates of a fraudulent sexuality.

Advertising certainly agrees that organism and environment are correlative.

People love to quarrel even with the dead.

A burn victim wants to claim greater knowledge than someone who avoided the fire.

Envy's need to bar any evidence other than flaws resembles the fetishist's need to bar any evidence other than shoes.

Bitter experience had taught him the futility of attempts accurately to sample his acquaintances' characters, and the amusement of deliberately inaccurate samples.

Fighters who have desensitized and brutalized themselves mock the effete indifference of philosophers.

Geniuses and con men say random data points are really continuous functions.

If romance and foreplay mattered that much to women they would not play with themselves.

Collective elephantiasis of the ego. The narcissist insisted that although his supposed enemy had not attacked anyone in several centuries, his situation was as morally acute as the Battle of Britain, because a great many of his relatives had been killed once upon a time by a European nation. Millions agreed that this ancient crime should be requited by annihilating an African nation.

Some sent orders contingent on impossibilities, or in undesirable currencies. Still others demanded research on aimless questions. Some did this with goods they had stolen themselves, to ensure futility.

Thirty pieces of nickel, Regimentsnickel. The amusement of intrigue turned out to be purely academic but the remorse all too practical.

She feigned benign indifference so well that he believed her, which she resented so much that she remained his nemesis long after he had given up altogether.

When you are going up against someone, budget lavishly and then quadruple it, since for them squandering your resources will be an end in itself. Then walk away from the quarrel.

Not having heard anything about him for ten years, they judged him by standards he had long ago vomited up.

If your opponent praises one aspect of something, make a fuss about some completely unrelated aspect. If he is winning in some abstract matter, raise doubts about his personality.

Nature insists the greatest success is irrelevant without reproductive advantage, and reproductive advantage is a trap.

Information gained by privacy invasion suboptimizes overall capital allocation by arbitrarily negating the victim's educational investment.

Women whose sexual technique is too advanced make you feel you are moderating final exams. Part of you is appalled to think you might as well leave a test dummy in your place and go for coffee, and part of you is charmed at the thought that it makes no difference at all whether your performance differs from any of your endless predecessors and successors.

Subhumanity delights in the apoplectic rage of the civilized men whose evidence is summarily discredited in the kangaroo court of the warmongers.

The movie is over and the credits roll on interminably; you should get up and leave, but there is a blizzard outside.

Hateful aggression posing as moderate decency frightened into posing as hateful aggression.

Jump from his partial concessions to the total conclusion.

When critical rationalism desiccates us it is sometimes worth rummaging around in animist myth for poetic fuel. What if disease is involuntary or unconscious yoga -- a pun cracked by our inner gremlin, as Groddeck thought, or a concentrated burst of incoming hatred?

Today Debs would have said that so long as falsely imprisoned men and women are robbed of sleep by their inquisitors he would remain an insomniac.

Freedom ordinarily means nothing more than the right to stand at a casino table. The larger freedom is the void where our actions are not painfully indifferent but utterly indifferent.

The intensity of some lesbians' desire to degrade the opposite sex can be found only in criminal males.

We become cowardly when we forget the perfectly good reasons why our instincts are not despicable. Would we really be ridiculed to death by parties unknown for things we would not even regard as faults in others? -- Yes, often enough.

The wages of sin is life; in injustice as everywhere else, long practice yields mastery.

Power lets a petty crook break into a million houses for the price of one.

Adults harden to the sight of psychopaths in public life as children do to amputees and burn victims.

How much veneration of Christ is semiconscious admiration of someone plucky enough to get on with suicide?

Life is a lock; evil need file away only a single ridge of the key.

A redneck who did not need to learn that virtue is often violence in disguise.

Polite Satanist education, incessantly fanning the flames of worldly craving and conflict, starving and vilifying virtue.

If the sanctity of motherhood is not a false value, why is it thought unable to triumph without the aid of the State?

Chinese revenge works only on people too lofty to deserve it.

Using strenuous exercise to push world-weariness over the brink prematurely is socialism in one organism.

When it comes to mathematics, the average teen suicide is two thousand years ahead of Socrates.

Why should the pricks be the only pricks? [ ] too likes to pass for intellect and justice. "If I'm not clever, then why do they pay me?"

Death is a coquette and the dreamscape is a glimpse of stocking.

If the mind must be caught in a squirrel wheel it should at least have maximum diameter.

Rest and oxygen can find an ounce of gold in a thought that an hour earlier was just a heap of dirt.

Her actual intentions were buried so deeply that you had to perform heavy signal processing on every response you elicited.

The game of fragments is about the second round, when you savage yourself in the persona of a rabbi or clown.

Newspapers give the mind paper cuts.

Truths so banal that you neglect to implement them. A huge mistake, but they are still banal.

Medicine can sometimes be close to certain a virus has been completely eliminated, but in psychotherapy cure is impossible by definition since latent relapses live in an area of the mind or brain defined as inaccessible to consciousness. Someone who really brought the id into the ego would spend all their time thinking about which ventricle to open, which drop of which hormone to release in which organ.

The cult of national security forgets murder is a sign of weakness.

A pity neurotics attacking their own projections have to damage the real people behind them.

Price movements in art are fluctuations in uncreative people's reaction to creativity. When the porn star pushed the price of an artwork past the price of a pretentious house, the world was filled with admiration for culture.

The bodybuilders who gain the most from the heaviest exercises are those born with the most muscle; spirituality has a similar capitalism.

New notation systems are good hunting for intellectual venture capitalists; one of them could prove the beginning of something like the merger of algebra and geometry. Until Gauss decreed otherwise in 1801, they used xx for x squared, and the entire nineteenth century overlooked Wessel's representation of complex numbers as vectors. With patents on numerical exponentiation and tractable orthogonality, you could take several penny commissions on every transaction ever made.

An unworthy enemy readily confuses disgusted with defeated silence.

Our vanity can make us repetitive bores but it sometimes saves us from premature disgust with our thoughts and virtues. They hung on the gallery walls for years without a buyer, but it turns out this was not our fault.

Journalism is virtuoso gossip.

Actions that brought us capital more than seven years ago were performed by an organism that no longer exists.

Beware of translating a dead author powerful enough to damage living interests; whether or not you agree with him, you are the target for retaliation.

It is absurd to suppose a consciousness created by nescience like the head of a boil should become the agent of liberation. But it is not absurd to suppose such a consciousness, dislocated by deeper forces, could accidentally stumble across the needle that can lance it.

Fast feminine recovery from embarrassment shows a better grasp of life as solipsistic lucid dream.

Voting blocs and their lobbyists: sickness, incompetence, doubt, delusion, sloth, indulgence, error, failure, unreliability, distraction, envy, cruel delight, malevolence, anger.

Envy indulges the sophistry condemned by the ancient Aryans, that cow-dung and milk pudding are the same because they both come from a cow.

Violent, diseducated dullards equip the electric guitar of their aggression only with one or two badly tuned bass strings; these cause the treble strings of the fully-equipped instruments around them to emit an unbearable cacophony of random harmonics. Deaf to their daemonic handiwork, uninterested in Humboldt, they blast everything out in the flatulent grandeur of D flat, convinced they have thereby scaled the heights of virtuosity. Is theirs not a remarkable piece of transposition, they ask. Does it not clearly vanquish and torment all the other keys? Is vanquishing and tormenting others at high volume not the true purpose of music? Would it not offend the Divinity were foreign keys to linger, posing a clear and present danger for the one true key? Is a man who writes in A not a philistine, a potential traitor?

Scolding a virus for being no gentleman.

While your conscience lives, loving your enemies and praying for those who spitefully abuse you is not compatible with loving your neighbor as your self, a self you would terminate in certain disgraces.

Other people's quest for glory is neurotic. If their goals were healthy they would not be outside our bodies.

Every worthwhile line of thought is a form of cowpox; you can suffer a long time from symptoms scarcely distinguishable from those it sets out to cure, and once they are gone you generally have little use for the medicine.

Making other people powerful means making them mistrust you.

The Christian graduate, headed out to disseminate black propaganda in a radioactive Teheran, dismissed the Persians as literally lunatics: did their ancestors not worship the Moon and the planets in their fire-temples? Was the temple where their Prophet died not called Mahdínah, Medinah, the place of the moon? Was it not the beautiful Casbah image of the moon that gave their chief shrine its name of Moon's Place, Máhgáh, Mecca? Well, yes, replied the defense lawyer, but in this were they not following Ibrahim, Abraham, "the friend of God", who destroyed all idols except those of the planets? Should we not perhaps step back in time, unshoot a few bullets, and figure out whether it was just laziness that omitted this critical exception from the competing scriptures? Why was Congress making a law establishing religious wars?

You are always being challenged to prove you do not know the bait is poisoned.

Descending into poverty means becoming accustomed to seeing not just your worldly goods but your personality and acquaintance in the light of imminent confiscation. Your virtues will soon be sold at auction.

Neurology has long had electrodes for rat pleasure centers and could mount a huge artificial satiation project to eliminate unfulfillable desires, but you would need mass sterilization to cope with the job losses.

Not all opium is opium of the masses.

Practical philosophy aims to turn apathy on and off at will.

The egotistical desire to dissolve the ego in favor of something better.

In the book of life we will find out how many hours we wasted on spurious questioning of our knowledge or probity.

Use subtly degrading definitions.

The government argued it must be forever exempt from scrutiny because it could not function were its advisors not free to give blatantly criminal advice.

He practiced intellectual fencing with an automatic gun.

Most men are more eager to dissociate themselves from their ugly bodies than from their ugly minds, but coarse sensuality and coarse idealism are the same road of samsaric dream.

A physicist complained that too many of his colleagues took hyper-idealism for granted: what is the point of dismissing materialism if it never attracted you in the first place?

Mortal hatred and immunodeficiency have similar latency periods.

Some positions exist for the sake of being dismissed, like incompetents hired to guard some bureaucratic flank.

Death could be the cellular analogue of the doubt which diffuses across the foundations of personality when we are rejected often or decisively enough without knowing why.

Slow suicide to escape reincarnation is a virtue; quick suicide to escape incarnation is a vice.

Bigots use divergent series expansions to prove the faults of their enemies infinite.

Strip that will to power of its silken humanitarian veil, the padded brassiere of utopian social engineering, the silk stockings of free enterprise, and you have a hideous hag whose folds of flab are scarcely distinguishable from her sagging breasts: Spite, the terminal cancer of egotism.

Two parts of ourselves condemn each other's reasoning; each claims to be the true self, both are lying visitors.

What happens in the mind of a child who learns his father might as well have been anyone else? Hitler's therapist found out after many years that at age 8 little Adolf had tossed and turned while his father was away on a business trip. He went outside to take the night air and found his once-sainted mama in the garden, complacently being [ ] by the greengrocer, a Jew.

We are so little different from those who came before us that we might as well be new versions of them, with a little added genetic salt or pepper. In fact we might as well be reincarnations of each other right now; no wonder we get along so badly.

Consciousness may not be able to grasp inner demons directly but it can scatter banana peels all over their walkway.

To make capitalism noble a perfectly informed world of unbounded rationality is necessary, but it is not sufficient: even a god may spend only because Olympian self-knowledge tells him he is an incorrigibly irrational wastrel.

The theory of karma is the most universal instinctive falsehood, constantly tracing prosperity back to some moral achievement which upon closer examination dissolves into egotism.

Her profession was demonstrating the inconsistency between reform and popular lies.

There are many idiotic mistakes we would never make were we not trying to help others with their idiotic mistakes. Some people have a genius for making us doze where we should be wide awake, for dissuading us from perfectly good ideas, for shoving us into situations it would never occur to us to enter, demanding our gratitude for the gratuitous humiliation.

To banish her childish boredom with table talk, she forced premature harvest after premature harvest from his mind until the soil was dangerously depleted.

An aggressive neurotic can sicken a healthy rival beyond repair, creating actual evidence for the game of "healthier than thou".

Achieving distance in the middle of an evil passion is easier than knowing which lesson to draw from it.

People habitually blamed for things beyond their control have that much less incentive to maintain control. If they are children, the shape of their identity takes on common walls with sadistic criticism and defenselessness.

Anger always rests on betrayal. One reason it is a deadly sin and scrupulously concealed by public figures is that the expectations betrayed are so often neurotic; Gresham's Law ensures that most viewers will automatically discount justified indignation to the level of narcissistic vindictiveness.

Obsessive pedagogic concern with a child's self-esteem can have silly side effects but surely its cruelest mockers do not fully understand how little they deserve the pain they cause.

Disillusionment is often pushed back on the genes and their sordid agenda, but why would the genes want to survive either if they can do so only as organisms whose most beautiful hopes are incoherent?

Friendships like curve sections that momentarily overlap and end up zagging off in opposite directions.

Faust says that if disaster is bound to happen, let it happen right away; half the sting of disease is the tantalizing glimpses of health it alternates with.

Simultaneously the greatest truth and the greatest lie ever told, possibly the sole political question: "No enjoyment is possible without injury to another entity."

The hormonal interpretation of Indian arguments against uninterrupted samsaric happiness is that you get higher emotional net profit from consistent levels than from the ignorant natural cycles, the way you get better efficiency bicycling at a constant speed. But you have to believe not only that the hormones can be brought under voluntary control but that you are the sort of organism that can manage it.

Much of what passes for concern about public health is no more sincere than the desire to protect the public health of the Massachusetts Bay Colony by wiping out the Indians all the way to California.

Some enemies would blush if they ever learned the damage they had inflicted on fronts irrelevant to their interests

After thorough contemplation of all the reasons for renunciation, after relentless battering from all the reasons for wallowing in worldliness, the battle-scarred self casts a crazy eye at both and vows one last stand against them. The universe did not come into being either for one pygmy to enslave another or for lunatics to play a guessing game of how they got tangled up in a straitjacket. God does not have to be a money-grubbing murderer or a purveyor of bad acid.

New books for spring. "Beyond Justice". "After Intelligence".

Part of you cannot ever quite accept that they would really stoop so low as to advocate asceticism or repression merely to cheat the competition. You want to believe there is some worthier reason, so you twist yourself in knots looking for worms in the loveliest apples. They have got the better of you by sheer crudity.

Some so-called felonies consist merely in demonstrating powerful people are more insipid than they can bear to be.

The yogi explained matter-of-factly that purification destroys the desire for "contact with women and children".

Contradicting everything in the hope of stumbling across a major fallacy: like schoolboys gambling on random answers in a multiple-choice test. This trick can briefly stun a good mind, since everything is vulnerable to doubt, if only in the sense that every lady is vulnerable to rape.

Renunciation reduces the number of suppliers who feel indebted for your custom.

How few our real needs are is obvious from how small a sum can seem infinite to so many, how easily it can create the illusion that common necessity has vanished from the earth.

If you become what everyone wants to be you become separate from what they can advise.

Resident aliens in a spiritual field look down at the tourist who has merely learned to read the language, but that does not make him a mere day-tripper. He may take the place less for granted than they do, and have more respect than his means allow him to demonstrate.

Fortunately it was exactly the sort of suffering needed to rinse the parabolic mirror of the mind and restore its solar concentration. They had hoped to block the gold with lead, which instead carried the dross away with it.

In the midst of the most idealistic philosophy there ever was, we find the postulate of a fixed substratum beneath matter, a rug under the furniture, put there only for the mental sensation it creates when you whip it out.

The devil may wish to present contemplation as nothing but bait for political apathy, but he cannot eliminate the existence of dreams and delta states: the victim's shoe may be tethered to poverty but he has long since left it and walked away.

Someone who hated a telepath would dump great truckloads of anger and lust into his mind.

Vague neurotic fear of losing control mocks paranoid or real fear of others' tyrannical whims.

Supreme concentration promises hypnotic powers such as invisibility, flight, entering other bodies, speech with animals. The desire for invisibility does not reflect confidence in the justice of either observer or observed.

Envious hate desperately desires the authority to cause iatrogenic disease.

What if the prohibition on perverse fantasy is nothing more than tarring true yogic concentration with the brush of false?

Some disasters feel as if we had once possessed a force not known to us but visible to an enemy who has now stolen it.

When we realize a wicked person has deliberately manipulated our affections part of the anger is over the energy wasted on the riddle of their wickedness.

Vice hopes that by degrading others to the level of its actions it can degrade them to its mental level.

Critics sneer at neurotics for lacking the placidity of dogs and pigs.

A judge who accepts entrapment evidence says the existence of a skeleton key is proof of an unsound lock.

To take advantage of waking dream powers you have to set yourself up for a disaster extreme enough to destroy your interest in anything else.

Existence could have passed the time arming our virtues but she seems to prefer pumping up our weaknesses.

America is so Jewish that even mentioning the existence of Jews as such can trigger defensive outrage. Ain't you heard of the Holocaust?

Is there a business school that teaches you how to recognize the brain areas that light up when a fool and his money are headed for the divorce courts? How about the brain areas for Pascal's wager, the ones that make people seriously wonder whether they are going to be punished with hellfire, or with reincarnation as a failed squid?

Business success walks across the hot coals of covetise.

For an infinite dramaturge the Divinity writes some remarkably insipid farces.

Odd to what lengths spiritual types can go to describe states of liberation that are as good as death, without embracing the real thing.

The circumstances and supporting cast might as well have been designed to blight love.

Objects in your physical world might as well be the ripening of latent impressions in your mind; existence is shadow-boxing.

To create symbolic respect for mathematics schools insist psychology students cover material which would not have been enough even at Alexandria.

She reproached him with passively waiting for inspiration, as if consciousness controlled the springs of thought and action.

A suddenly impoverished man is a midair diver without a diving board or pool.

Sade took into the drawing room what the others try to conceal in the outhouse of war and prison.

An underreported part of youth wasted on the young is the lesson of parental hate and indifference.

Critics of our mental decor, nauseated by the dog mess they themselves left on our rug.

How many clever people have been stifled by excessive awareness of the odds against their cleverness being as great as their vanity would have it?

Sidetrack an argument headed for your defeat.

Muslim fanatics deny this is an era where political women aim to eliminate inequity rather than usurp it; not merely to obtain, but to deserve money and position; to dispense with intrigue altogether.

Thoughtless bigotry dismissed the idea as thoughtless bigotry.

Success has to be on your own and has to be with other people's resources.

Guilty people want adultery to be nothing more than a trivial incursion on illegitimate or neurotic property claims, petty theft from an overflowing public well; but one might as well reduce arson to burglary; a petty thief does not breach genetic contracts reaching endless generations into the future, nor usurp the right to assess the penalty for fraud in the Platonic search, or to condemn another as too base to distinguish between intimacy and property.

Every fly has his dunghill.

Critics who dismissed Flaubert and Debussy as randomizers were unequal to a problem in induction.

He wrenched the fetus from the womb, leaving blood all over the floor, and brandished it at a press conference. It was as he had thought, her vices had almost led to deformed infants.

He disapproved of the death penalty while endorsing unprovoked war. Non-murderers deserved extermination, murderers forgiveness.

Not knowing their attack vector, he spent a billion on a Maginot Square.

Humiliation causes a downward hormonal spiral, internal feedback far beyond diminishing returns, more like a pulled muscle than a workout burn.

Give your subjects arms so they will feel like your soldiers instead of your suspects.

Broad education plus stern conscience equals scholarly neurosis. You embarrass history and yourself by ascribing a thought to a nineteenth- rather than a twelfth-century pedant; but he world could not care less which is which; it does not need such details to judge itself wiser than Plato, more revolutionary than Robespierre, and pay itself accordingly.

An economist who had apparently spent too much time in the company of women said that if you do not compete for wealth you are automatically an ontological second-rater. This works if you stop at Thales, but are we to believe Newton had Virginia plantations and Einstein was obsessed with bond yields?

When our good angel deserts us we want to say: look, you are the angel, not us; you knew very well about the seeds of motive for whatever it was we did to displease you; all you had to do was give us the nod and we would have refrained; surely abandoning us now is impossibly harsh; what sort of angel are you, anyway? And the angel says: I was not your good angel, I only helped you to hurt someone else and they are gone, goodbye. Or: sorry, it was a game of Job and I was forbidden to speak. Or: get a grip, angels do not exist.

Even after the earth is wholly industrialized people will find excuses to fly around it. You will be able to transfer any information you might desire to any point on the globe; your correspondent will be able to watch your face; your surgeon will operate remotely; yet the flying around will never cease. People will do anything to achieve a false sense of great scope. Those who have seen through the trick complain about always being stuck in airports, but only some are sincere.

99% of their surface area was the same but their cusps did not match, so they mortally offended one another.

No need to discard a metaphor like 'mental illness' simply because idiots have taken it too literally. However skeptical we are about the purported cures there is no gainsaying the feeling that certain ideas have infected the mind and caused a terrible rash, even eaten flesh. Gargantuan doses of spite can achieve this effect, the way gargantuan loads of bombs can poison the water whether or not they kill the inhabitants.

Intellectual promiscuity risks exhausted bigotry.

He went to bed in a severe depression, woke her up at three with a fit of laughter he never knew about, and rose at seven with a morning erection.

Their strength can blind you to their philistinism.

If you taught a child to fill a notebook with every contradiction it observed, by the time it left home you would have endless pages of personal foibles and superficial paradoxes, but laced with enough raw material for a new La Bruyère.

Indifference is not there for the taking as some philosophers suggest; it is a finite resource; some people cannot afford it; others have so much it gives them a kind of gout.

Hostile tempests want to argue their lightning has such powerful voltage it must be enlightenment.

The urge to return to society springs from the illusion that the detachment of exile can live on to triage the turmoil of business.

Argue that 95% of worldly goods are illusory and the world may pretend you are refuted by its withholding of the remaining 5%.

A book that writes itself too easily is open to the same suspicions as a young person who adapts too readily to intrigue.

The chance for complete rebirth is always five inches away but usually along an inaccessible axis.

Better a serious enemy than a jocular traitor.

When reason betrays us we are tempted to gamble on the spontaneous subconscious. But it was the subconscious that trashed reason in the first place; has it finished its fun, or does it intend to kill us?

Authors have their seasons; Mandeville is more amusing at the top of a business cycle than in the bread line.

Until society loses all zero-sum aspects, people who reproduce above replacement will be committing aggression against others and will band together like all aggressors, asserting a nonexistent right to push other people aside, or to depress their wages by making laborers less rare.

So few people could bring us a fraction of the happiness we have from the harmless errors they would be able to point out.

Philosophers have always complained that their age is obsessed with money as never before. There has always been someone to explain that excessive individualism has finally arrived at the verge of eliminating the family; that knowledge is an inch away from completely mirroring the universe. The boys who cried wolf -- but the wolf did show up in the end.

Do not let the sword of Damocles rush you to oblige those who want to see you thrust through. They will have plenty of time to relish your destruction; take as much pleasure as you can from the intervening moments.

The clue to advantage over someone is knowing which variables he treats as constants. Fallen man thinks every such mistake is partial differentiation.

Once upon a time some clever old man must have been so relieved to find himself pushed off the roller-coaster of love that he hypnotized the young men into thinking going to bed with girls was not really any fun.

There are so many things to harden yourself against that you are almost certain to overdo it at some moment and trample what you would have cut your finger off to save. This is likely to be more interesting than many of your other deeds, and thus to stain your reputation more deeply if luck does not offer you a perfect excuse.

Make sure that when your enemy is put to the test you have configured the test for some territory that he did not claim but that viewers can be led to believe he might have claimed. This lets you fabricate evidence of incompetence tinged with a false shadow of fraud which will not be dispelled until long after the damage is done, if at all.

Ridicule trumps truth.

A cunning female shamed her rivals for their despicable failure of empathy toward the victims of a sinister plot she had secretly authored.

History shows brilliant and productive men mocked all their lives, expending superhuman energy to defeat some blatant lie, their editions remaindered, their bodies hauled off to the scaffold; this is supposed to have ended now because of fast communications; how could we know?

In ruin the sense of time dissolves and we become ghosts in our own lives. Once we wanted to escape the illusion of time; well, here we are, off the leash, obliviated. Envy, lust, competition also dwindle, leaving a polite residue lest we devalue others' prizes and plans. When formerly finite demands on our resources become infinite, resentment eventually gives way to irony: so this is the outcome of so much political progress; very well, here, take the rest. Yet we continue taking exercise, writing business, going into society, half grateful no one notices we do not really exist any longer. They may have made up the part about being reborn in Christ, but the dying-to-yourself bit is not bad.

If he were a book there would be coffee stains and cigarette burns all over it, marginalia, a weak cover, nothing but text.

Unless your enemy habitually takes low blows, be flattered when really overwhelming force has to be mustered against you.

One weekday afternoon you wander into a junk shop in a small California town. Upstairs, amid cheap porcelain and dreadful paintings, are books shelved in chaotic disorder. You look at failed novelists of a hundred years ago, who might as well be newspaper writers of the day; at textbooks from forgotten schools, ratty library copies of Augustine or Rousseau, a sensational pulp exposé of a scandal from before the birth control pill, a question and answer book for obscure parish priests just after the Great War, mid-century women's sex novels, treatises on some bureaucratic corpse, thirty-year-old gossip magazines that make you wonder whether the actresses are still alive in some geriatric ward. The sun gets a little lower and you light a cigarette for one of the endless ashtrays; there are no other customers to complain, the management would not care if there were. -- You have had almost enough of literary mortality and mediocrity when you come across an author you have never heard of, with a title betraying the higher literary dilettantism. The first few glances confirm your suspicion that he managed to bypass most of the pressing nothings of his day. He is a little too preoccupied with authors but his respect is not inane; he clearly recognizes the historical burden of proof for real originality, and tries for it without rubbing your nose in the sweat. No one heard of this man in his day except some vainly prescient editor, and no one will again; he was not quite strong enough to wrench himself into history. But he did strike you with one brilliant sentence that is to make you, possibly his sole posterity, unimaginably rich. You make your way down the stairs, past the absurd profusion of deceased clocks and jewelry, and buy the stock of the century, all of it, for the price of a newspaper.

Sloth is the cheap cynicism of the body.

Perpetual suicide approaches the detachment of genius, to no avail.

Some truths can be revealed only by the lies they contradict.

Make sure you hit the wall fast enough to die immediately!

The judge ruled that the extenuating circumstances were just artifacts of the image enhancement algorithm the lawyer had used on her client.

The comic hallucination of free will: a transparent toilet on a transparent floor above an airport customs office. Turns out the State does not expect as much moral agency from suspects as the criminal law would suggest. And yet the suspects do remain continent from time to time. One man made it through the three days only to have one of his heroin bags burst just afterwards. There was time for the Professor to flush him out, but he was never intelligently miserable again.

All right, we tried to get rid of it but it won't go away.

Pride yourself on grasping what others cannot and you may end up like an algebraic geometer who has missed a far more elegant synthetic proof.

Her career was shoving others into degrading reference frames.

Children assume you can dispose of notions like virtue and modernity as you would dispose of old tissues.

Huge minds take us to pristine desert islands on faraway planets; ordinary leadership offers a package holiday, a stuffed jet, a crowded beach, an overdeveloped resort.

Bábá Nânac reassembled cows, horses and elephants from the stomachs of the crowds who had devoured them. Perhaps he could tell us how to recover our Constitution from our creditors.

Politicians extolling the dignity of labor while attacking the minimum wage should be compelled to roll up their sleeves and put their money where their mouth is. This would be even more amusing were prostitution legalized.

Perfect copying machines make original artworks and first editions obsolete ways of conflating money and taste.

Cheerily dissolving shame in collective guilt is a mark of mediocrity.

Having pestered him relentlessly for inspiration and correction she noticed he had ended up spending a disproportionate time in her presence and concluded that he was suffering from a morbid dependence on her. It must have been some virtue of her own that had entitled her to presume on his courtesy. As the strains hidden elsewhere in his life sapped his ability to bear the sight of her forever playing the mandolin in filched and ill-fitting finery, he withheld the free bons mots until she decided there must be no major veins left to exploit. Had there been any there in the first place, or had she only projected them, out of the fulness of her grace, to give this poor typist a chance to bask briefly in her radiance? He was after all hopelessly in love with her, more than happy to be dragged out of his orbit any time ten seconds of solitude had left her frantically bored and thirsty for a convenient distilled dose of the new events and ideas she was too lazy to tackle on her own. Discipline was for more important matters: redecoration, hostessing, occasional bouts of decorative painting to maintain a presence in the fashion magazines.

Make sure your subordinates' flaws disqualify them for your job.

As a devout American he was disturbed about usurping the Creator's prerogative of genetic manipulation, unless it be through the use of radioactive mass destruction weapons.

Hatred as emergency glue for the personality.

At a party a stockbroker instructed me that nihilism was the doctrine of teenage resentment. He said he had learned this from Nietzsche. He had transcended it by impregnating a woman, thus leaving the animal realm behind.

The coefficients of crisis yield no roots at all, let alone real ones.

Politicians' superior intuitive grasp of human nature makes them not superior philosophers but superior madams. A bribe is not an argument, a blow job is not a concept.

The poetical and philosophical heroes of the past confront their contemporary competitors every day, and live to tell the tale. Would Meyer Rothschild and his coin-collection sales spiel cut anything like as good a figure competing with today's traders? What is the financial analogue of intellectual immortality?

Each generation needs some character assassination of its predecessors if its reputation is to achieve critical economic mass and its intellectual retailers are to pass for manufacturers.

Curing diseases before they are detected means curing our own projections.

Ignorance is as real a commodity as soybeans. Without it who could demand a bar of gold for something he just acquired for a bar of lead? Credulity too is an elixir one can freeze into the mad ice sculpture of a financial cathedral.

Sporus insists he has free will, because the particles in his brain are indeterminate quanta. Welcome to Monte Carlo.

Break faith when the original rationale no longer holds.

A minimum-security prison is a gallery of those vices whose full significance has made a lucky escape from the masses and their representatives.

Force and fraud want you to believe they won a fistfight rather than an armed robbery. But whether it is an over-informed trader a lady confronts, or a punk with a shotgun, it is the machine that takes away her purse.

A master of the lie argued that exploitation was ultimately impossible because any victims of oligarchy or oligopoly could simply change suppliers, change employers, as did Bruno and Vanini and the other heretics and Jews dissatisfied with the Church's product line during the Inquisition.

Critique of causality and synchronicity. One stranger lies to another; the pocketbooks of a lawyer and stockbroker and doctor swell; the national wealth has grown.

A truth becomes makes itself useful as a polygon and we complacently forget we cross-sectioned it from a polytope.

Try to come to power through the many rather than the few. You will have fewer rivals once in power and your constituents will just want to be left alone rather than anger others.

Life is neither continuous nor everywhere differentiable nor dimensionally static.

He reproached himself for not stating a sober truth as a cynical pun.

Occam's razor is an intellectual antibiotic losing its edge in the incessant multiplication of incurable desires.

Forbid a weak enemy time to regroup.

Yogic masochism is the most thorough hardening of malice's target. Sade was a black yogi of sorts, his outrages against the pathetic hope of mutual love and kindness a slathering preemptive strike against disillusionment.

If the ideology of unfettered competition were true there could be no family that would not grow perpetually stronger through domestic surveillance, gunfights, affairs. Spouses would be toning themselves up for the defense of a free society.

A thriller about a detective whose efforts bring crippling self-consciousness, bankruptcy and death to a basically innocent person forced into a crime out of unjust desperation.

The neurotic defense mechanisms of the state need to obscure their role in the damage they cause. Someone realistically and acutely aware of its perverted intrusive surveillance has to be smeared as mysteriously inhibited and indecisive.

One of the great consolations of artificial reality would be the ability to indulge in the life-lies our consciences presently only permit our adversaries.

How much time we could save did we see immediately how much of someone's happiness is feigned.

They were able to refute all her proofs of the truth.

Each age has its immortal innovation in jargon: forms, substances and accidents, epicycles, ether. We have Dawkins' Meme (and its louche second cousin the Engram), a Platonic parasite shaping our brain blob to suit its fancy. Ours too is the Network, with its fib that nerves work the same way as silicon chips doing real arithmetic to find the second derivatives of error functions.

Arguing that all pensioners can get rich on the stock market amounts to arguing that everyone can absorb the same losses.

Fashion makes us overly uncharitable about our grandparents' jargon. Today psychiatry finds talk of a "death instinct" hopelessly quaint, though every cigarette smoker knows it is perfectly good poetry about the hidden parts of the mind content with the devil's bargain.

Matchmaking service question #435: what sort of secret do you find unbearable?

The effort to provide someone electronically with a better net ratio of comfort and despair than heroin would be as big as the effort to develop atomic weaponry. The Divinity's gift of heroin to German chemistry was the same hint he offered when Tibetan Buddhism emerged from the poppy fields of Afghanistan: if you keep working you will eventually be able to blunt your stupid desires by manipulating yourselves rather than trashing my Garden.

Courtesy misled him into allowing enough dubious premises to kill him with a false conclusion.

There is something you do not know you have. You would be happy to give but you are not asked. You are condemned as illiberal.

Other people are forever taking the easy way out.

The spite and envy at the root of prohibitions on recreational drugs is so disproportionate that one is surprised more of it has not spilled over into angry prohibition of antibiotics, crutches, toothpaste.

Modesty starts out well enough, reminding us that something else hath made us and not we ourselves, but it risks the inability to imagine an audience supportive enough to sustain creative morale.

Sometimes we can provoke ourselves to action only by psychological warfare against ourselves, demonizing an internal enemy into a sulfur-breathing alien.

She did not know he had never really left her, nor grasp that her heart was broken.

The neurotic love of consistency upholds society as gnomes uphold the academic standing of a class.

Mathematics and poetry are endless games of substitution. If you fill a curve with enough polygons to approximate the area you eventually get to the calculus.

All right, have it your way, laments about the world's falsehood depend on an illegitimate postulate of a true world. But this does not make the impulse to truth any less natural a fact than your strategic narcissism.

We should be satisfied with genetic inequality because randomness is basic; we should assume free will because there is indeterminacy in models of atoms; but we must assume strict meritocratic determinism in wealth distribution.

A traitor soils every similar relationship you have, since consistency obliges you to discount them all at the same rate applied to your debased faith in your judgment.

Force a false choice between caricatures.

"Imagine your legs were taken away in a horrible practical joke…"

Forced to hurt someone she loved for the sake of someone she owed, a tacit and usurious debt poisoning all of life.

The truth would have made them both happy but he was forced to play dumb.

The devil enjoys making us waste resources criticizing what is beneath criticism.

The body stopped accepting the mind's promissory notes.

Dread of pornography is dread at the flimsiness of our individuality. What sort of God worth having would make our affections mere probability densities, while leaving us the need for so many certainties?

By the end of the twentieth century blacks and Jews were taboo prey and communists an endangered species. Drug users and perverts had to carry the whole witch hunt. Next it will be the Little Green Men.

Some remarks are profound only because they sprang from an unknown personality. Affected taciturnity tries to capitalize on this.

Someone interrupting you with a spurious decision request is a flashing red light: warning, the devil wants false evidence of your inattentiveness.

Indecency is burglary of the unconscious, the holy grail of consumer communications analysis.

One judge of national character is the size of the statute books. Laws are the fossils of injustice.

Only need can motivate the poor, said the capitalist, and only status can motivate the rich, so neediness and snobbery must forever remain the fountainhead of economic endeavor.

If readers of maxims are lazy then so are users of mathematical formulas and machines. Many theorems would not be worth using if you had to scrutinize their proofs.

Politicians are the spirochetes of intellectual life, using money as the virus uses its false chemical passport.

Mediocre cleverness knows the easy 51 percent of truth yields more than the hard 49.

Government by scientific polling is rape of scientific method's contempt for instinct.

Her conversation was as rich as a cake with too much butter.

Each lie reproaches the other with irrationality.

The mob prefers the artist unaware he is derivative.

Overly aggressive salesmanship confesses unworthy goods or customers or both.

Bad conscience pretended it was just playing a comedy.

Keep your nobles satisfied but not at popular expense.

Artificial reality machines are pushbutton yoga.

Privilege confuses complacency with objectivity, as if self-satisfaction were the cornerstone of empiricism.

Some optical illusions have multiple interpretations, some turn out on closer inspection to have no interpretation. The first is pluralism, the second Buddhism.

Persecution of altered mental states proclaims the failure of philosophical and religious education.

Con men fascinate because they hint at the absurdity of all ambition.

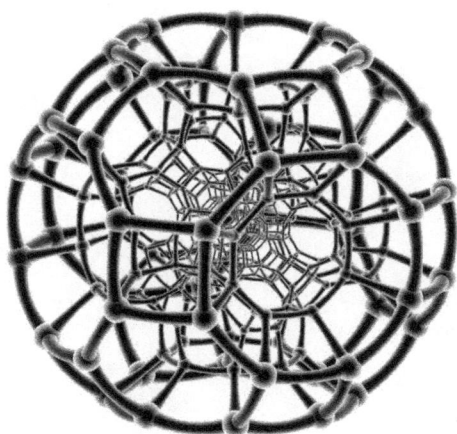

A capricious fate has decreed that all the millions of people due to die today will depart life from your city. The electricity is still flowing but on the subway platform and in the cars are thousands of corpses you must step over to operate the train. You arrive at the stock exchange floor to find the screens flashing wild price swings above a heap of dead traders.

Love sometimes brings flowers to the grave of lust, where we might otherwise be tempted to spit.

Under strict representation an official voted into office by 14% of the electorate could receive up to 86% of the punishment for murder committed in the name of the State.

Take Christian principles seriously enough to neglect your body irreversibly and you will marvel at the animal hypocrisy of the well-fed moralists who pump the jails full.

Those who criticize romantic love as neurotic immaturity glorify the limits of their imaginations. We are already condemned to live in a world of mutual projections; fidelity would change the movie rather than the screen.

Genius and oblivion. A lady went mad with schizophrenic outrage over the relentless intrusions of a worldwide surveillance network. Her daughter, who had ample reason to pity her delusion, lived to see this network come into existence thirty years after her mother's death.

Get cruelties out of the way promptly but stretch out kindnesses.

Sometimes a petty humiliation is harder to ignore than a real defeat, because it makes us vulnerable to a pettier range of criticisms; the worst ancient torture was simply to coat the victim with milk and honey and let the flies drive him mad.

You say something wicked out of boredom or impatience and are horrified later to find it was the truth.

A mental Lilliputian, industriously sucking vitamins from its patch in the intestinal wall of intellectual history, thought it regal comedy to mock a manifesto of the desperate poor as a novel.

Most vacancies would not yet exist if their occupants had continued to tolerate the slot.

Conversation with too much garlic: delicious but stinky afterwards.

What greater good would be served if the races completely reversed their social positions?

Compound interest on sleep debt is as ruinous as any other. Foul moods and weakness are the penalties, immune disorders the bankruptcy petition.

The indifference of the ignorant public is harsh but one might fare even worse were everyone clever and free enough to flood the market with high-quality art and push the price of genius through the floor.

Why would a Supreme Being not create diseases that left us laughing rather than sniffling in our beds?

Eccentrics have a different notation system for morals. They seem to be struggling with cuneiform when they could be using base ten. Sometimes this is because we are the cuneiform users and cannot pose the problems in their superior notation.

Some indiscretions could never happen if only we were rude enough to tolerate an embarrassing silence.

A first-rate pedant began studying women and fashion; he turned into a Restoration fopling with footnotes.

Indifference to the sincerity of compliments: we need not be vain enough to credit their source, merely relieved at a moment of non-aggression.

As life progresses and our interests grow more complex it is less and less likely that our best qualities will pop up at the same time as the need for them, or that the reward for the virtue will be available anywhere near the time we renounce the vice.

People who advise calm concentration in the face of impending ruin are like the muscle-men who guarantee fitness if you do a million barbells a day.

Some laziness has to be unconscious resistance to something other than labor, dread of some outcome not consciously sensed.

The demand that one become as a child is not just about innocence. If we are making progress it grows harder for others to give us the fascinating illusion of novelty. Stagnation maintains our sincere pleasure in their achievements and their sincere relief at our inferiority.

If intelligence were a good in itself paralysis would be a virtue.

IQ numbers are intercepts of complicated curves.

Discovering someone in the same unmentionable trap as you is a second cousin of falling in love.

To prevent her bigotry from becoming solidly unconscious she reduced it to absurdity with private vitriol.

Personalities operate on one another like waves. Some amplify and beautify each other's peaks and troughs, but as life grows more crowded there are more and more possibilities for white noise.

Intellectual arbitrage: by endorsing the orthodox multiple earths and heavens and hells of the anonymous Muslim, Bruno became a renegade, immortal martyr of empiricism.

The tightrope. If you fail to simulate the prole religion the proles become restive. If you succeed too well, you proletarianize yourself beyond redemption. And once you use force there is no telling whether there will be anything left in the end but force.

Every nation falsifies every other's lazy assumptions about the inevitability of its arrangements, opening even their shared traditions to doubt.

Unjust advantage likes to see hatred as envy.

Tibetan dream yoga calls on both guru and dakini, Yezdanian guru yoga on a more abstract Instructor, or even on the mirror image of the practitioner himself. Does minimizing the cultural determination of the guru image, even conceiving it as an alternate self rather than an Other, speed access to the unconscious or slow it down?

When a person internalizes oppression it is called neurosis. When an impoverished nation does it there is talk of adaptation and competitiveness.

A politician asked for my money on the grounds that we both supported abortion. This has happened once too often. If I am going to be dunned for commercials belaboring the obvious, they should at least be about the beauty of sunsets or the delectability of Italian sorbet.

Rarely are we sufficiently ashamed at the coarseness of the link between our interests and opinions.

Today someone who had murdered 1000 civilians indicted someone else as a war criminal, claiming they had murdered 350. Does this ratio appear elsewhere in moral nature? Is there a Golden Section of hypocrisy?

Faint praise sprinkled like sugar in a fuel tank.

Violence likes to steal everything, even the mantle of disinterested scholarship. How can one pass for king of the barbarians if one tramples only bodies?

Among us the phrase "overprivileged virago" is a contradiction in terms, but I have heard that somewhere in the South Atlantic there is an island where females are said to have vices and even to intend their husbands more damage than the Muslims do their wives, who are explicitly entitled to orgasm by their Scripture.

In a just society the man who proposed poor bachelors and spinsters bankroll babysitters for rich brood sows would be pelted with eggs.

A messy love triangle, three simultaneous equations in only two variables.

Play on the fear of a reputation for ingratitude.

A sober married woman laughing in her illicit consort's face for worrying about contraception. The voice of the species laughing at individual obstacles to its diktat.

Religious bigots are right to suspect yoga as ultimately hostile to the physical ideal of the healthy stud or mare. Yoga as health kick is a Big Cheery Lie, since the ancient purpose of yoga asanas is to destroy identification with the body. Hatha Yoga is the self-destruction of the botched will by other means. So is Christianity, so are certain vices.

A female ruler who oversaw half a million vice convictions and the greatest expansion of intrusive surveillance in history demanded her husband have the right to lie in court about his mistresses.

Electronic communication will have done its dubious job when cybernetic sex causes physical indifference between the sexes.

Kissing reality goodbye, the Judas kiss.

We do not know what our friends really like about us, so we also do not know exactly why they cut us. Sometimes we apply our greatest virtues to create what in their eyes is a downfall.

You can get accustomed to very high doses of nicotine and turn them to advantage stimulating the nerves. Malice too can keep you alert. But it is more likely to resemble small daily doses of cyanide in your coffee.

Infatuation had so invigorated her that evening that she sparkled more than she knew. Her brilliant remarks unwittingly and falsely implied he had been catastrophically deceived; being intelligent enough to appreciate her, he went stone cold; she began to think him a rather dull fellow after all; Nature laughed satanically at the abortion of love.

If you are too stupid to refute someone, try to enrage him into indiscretion, or idly contradict him until he exaggerates in exasperation.

Mechanical innovations are beloved partly because they pay off the debts accrued by intellectual laziness. You are cleverer than your betters, because what they worked to achieve you get simply by pressing a button.

If you cultivate an impression of being not quite clever enough to take a subtle hint, or not quite normal enough to sleep with girls, or not quite practical enough to fight, you may lull your enemy with self-flattery but you must expose his arrogance before slander sinks in.

Diligent hypocrisy despises idle frankness. Amply rewarded mediocrity scolds starving apathy.

If confiding a conscious secret makes you vulnerable to the Chinese whispers of your friends' friends, how much more indiscreet to confide a dream, where your unconscious may confess motives you would easily censor. The ancient Persian kings more than once beheaded, or allowed their children to behead, subjects who had experienced disloyalty in dream or trance.

A position is a grimace leaving characteristic wrinkles in the mind.

Malice, envy, greed, romantic love and hate can be desperate simulations of mental focus.

The social universe expands too; everyone progresses along a vector with a different number of dimensions; an inverse square law of attraction lessens the attractions between us until even our cells are no longer interested.

A sudden epidemic of hostility, grounded in impure sources and vile methods it is ashamed to reveal, like a woman flaunting a pregnancy begun with a series of acts she would be mortified to see on film. Characters too tangential to be in on the plot suddenly inspire our gratitude, as if their obliviousness were conscious courage against a raging storm.

The line between philosophy and pedantry in the Indians is the line between vindaloo paste and raw asafetida powder.

We reproach the ancient Indians for their rabid misogyny, accusing them of projecting their own chaos onto the sexuality of women, but they were just anticipating you, Bathsheba.

Choosing the lesser political evil over hopeless purity is mature only where the lesser evil includes no absolute evils.

Make the enemy think he is achieving something by refuting the opposite of what you want him to concede.

A sophist who could transform any useful expression into a divergent series.

Only psychopaths know the full pleasure of the theory that all publicity is good publicity.

Conventional decency insists the id circle be squared with ruler and compass.

When misfortune has dazed us, poured water on our candle, we may undervalue the past evidence of our virtues as a way station on the road to disaster, and write them off instead of using them as the most natural fresh start.

Love grows crystals on barren branches in intellectual life too. Nietzsche nourished his militaristic thought experiments on one of Vauvenargues' duller sentiments: the soldier's life-lie about perpetual war as a cure for softness. Military softness is a vice in soldiers, not civilians.

To a kid with an elliptic curve everything is crypto.

A Talmudist informed me after dinner that Mary was a neighborhood slut who made up the tale of the Angel to dupe her husband. In exchange I was to understand that the Diaspora was involuntary, the Khazars of Eastern Europe the legitimate heirs of North African land, and American taxes well spent exporting the most sophisticated weapons to the Land of Israel for sale to Oriental enemies.

Indian indifference: If the dentist will never come, you brush your teeth but you also prepare for the day when you must be completely oblivious to toothache. If you are ready a little early, so much the better.

From the ubiquity of vice religion prematurely concludes omnipresence; from the venality of a corrupt Church the critique of religion prematurely concludes the Commandments are pure swindles.

Anger forgets its enemy will eventually get the death penalty anyway.

Most everyone ends up practicing yoga involuntarily, since the body ends up the playground of some dark force we can no longer identify with; this destroys the habit of identifying with our thoughts.

No matter how long the series of ideas and impulses that arises in the mind, and no matter how well it fits the market, they are natural eruptions, like thunderstorms, which do not own or merit anything. One may declare oneself entitled to reduce other people to factors of production if circumstances permit, but thieves are doing the same; they merely drive the particularly harsh bargain of zero wages. What Proudhon really meant was "theft is the reductio ad absurdum of property".

A universal genius with not a single moment to savor the fruits of the infinite worldly wisdom he showered on others. Even greater genius would have savored the world more and left posterity only the bare minimum for indisputable immortality.

Attribute nonexistent quotes to authorities your opponent cannot judge.

If there were such a thing as a just war Christ would have aborted the Crucifixion and wiped out his accusers.

Man cannot be the malicious animal because the cat has already mastered the art. Every formula for human uniqueness is as marginal as our genetic uniqueness.

Scholars who treat the great minds like steroids lose their intellectual liver.

Misery #494: being forced into a professional role you care little enough about and are rewarded little enough for that your concentration decays. Some aggressor will soon smell profit in representing this role as your entire self, a self he is superior to because he has invented it.

A demagogue with good instincts for the highest common denominator of the masses automatically gives the misleading impression that he will rise higher at the first opportunity.

High literature is the pornography of the soul.

Desire is lack; the worldliest manipulator is the most effective at what remains lacking once money and sex are solved.

Obsession: the scantier the data set, the more curves the imagination fits to it.

Poor people are more generous because gifts do not threaten to bleed their riches.

Betrayal shocks because our allies are supposed to be part of ourselves, and that makes them in some part objects, like a foot you stare down upon from up in the skull. The amputation mutilates your body image. You are supposed to be able to walk on the foot and give it an occasional blister without waking up one morning to find it halfway across the room on another body with more comfortable shoes.

Overprivileged ignorance wants to be sovereign contempt.

Many moral problems require the same kind of substitutions that dissolve insoluble integrals.

Severe damage to our self-esteem makes everyone seem more aggressive.

Vices are hard to break because they date from some time when the only sure and cheap way to get meditative relaxation came with some terrible string attached. The cheapness remains, virtue is just as tenuously rewarded, the string tightens.

People seem more intelligent when they have shared our misfortunes, half-baked if their consciences have never risen to whatever level tortures us.

The moment he was sure the mental well had dried up was the only moment she ever admired his wit.

Interest too crudely feigned offends more than indifference.

Many lies are told more reluctantly than it seems, out of misplaced sense of duty to a role.

She used skepticism like a little boy uses a hammer.

When a determined enemy manages to open old wounds you can weave a fast bandage by focusing on malice's need for attention.

Torture attempts to prolong the orgasm of hatred.

Severe disease can illuminate more than intellectual exercise, but that does not guarantee much light.

Pretentious nonsense works best against a pretentious enemy.

How could an illiterate Hindu hope to waste as much energy on idols as governments do on the magical images of wargaming machines?

Ruined by a one-percent rise in the interest rate.

If salvation is release from the evils of finite egotism then it is a cousin of despair.

Our own minds contain spies collecting secret dossiers. When we finally get access to the file we find obsolete thought patterns have left behind all sorts of idle libels.

"We admit our policy was nothing more than a wicked pretext to steal public money."

A teacher passed around a test with fifty hard questions, the last of which was a command to ignore the questions and submit an empty sheet of paper. - What if the real challenge of life is to grasp and act upon its pointlessness the fastest? What if child suicides achieve the greatest possible net happiness?

No amount of priestly cunning could have made religion so powerful if independent thought were rarely a torment.

We escape a thousand manipulators only to fall prey to some forgotten childhood scam.

Assert your conclusion triumphantly as if its premises had not been voided.

Pettiness besets an overstrained mind as viruses do an exhausted body.

Evil people enjoy mocking the conscience that prohibits the retaliation they deserve.

Lully lullay: Body and mind are bad dreams.

Unjustly thwarted desires are hardest to uproot.

Libertines give the lie to the hope that satiation might be the express train to cheery disillusionment and detachment.

When you are in extremis you always run across someone who prescribes an elementary dose of something that helped get you into your mess. You should be as diligent as you were during project X, which earned you the enmity of half your friends.

A child who has just completed Apollonius is cocky towards the man who has long since discovered Apollonius does not pay.

You have to destroy satellites too accustomed to liberty.

Committing great crimes with impunity must encourage the feeling that the physical world is as much a dream as the moral. Here you stand, having broken the most sacred laws of God and man, and the world is still going its merry way: perhaps the victims really were stick figures and you can do as you please?

Pedants envy the vulgarizer who got the point so cheaply; journalists envy the pedant who would not settle for rhinestones.

Big lies die down when their partisans run short of blood money.

Insufficient challenge -- boredom -- carelessness -- inhumanity.

Walking diffidently after your legs have been sawed off is not cowardice.

If you palm yourself off as a fawning dog no one will begrudge you the ability to smell a rat at ten thousand paces.

Her vanity turned out to be strictly defensive.

The desire to govern others varies directly with the monstrosity of our ability to govern ourselves.

If you starve someone you will soon be able to accuse them of coarse obsession, with food or money or sex or drugs; if they bear up under your torture you can claim their passions are paltry.

The Inquisition too was peer review.

There are capitalists who would like to pretend their critics and skeptical friends simply do not understand the fun of bossing people around and having a big party. They are like Auden's middle-aged man celebrating his bowels.

Baldly imply that your incomprehension implies the adversary's pretentiousness.

Someone hoping to discover truth among men should reflect how many parents lie to their children about their intemperance and love affairs, and how much money the government spends to back them up. If children can do 17th-century mathematics perhaps they can also do 17th-century morals, perhaps even benefit from the advice of the trade group which best understands the business of love.

Hate can be the mind's attempt to catch up with reality: the animal self thinks infinite mistrust might forestall the write-off from misplaced confidence.

If you must be liberal, tout your generosity so you will at least avoid false accusations of stinginess. Localize meanness, generalize liberality.

Cowardice likes to see itself as prudence, even wisdom, but no amount of algorithmic sophistication can make it courageous to launch an invisible attack on a defenseless adversary.

Even an exhausted mine yields gold on those rare occasions when you can tunnel to a virgin vein on the other side of the earth.

Ordinary rudeness can briefly take on the flavor of psychotherapy; therapeutic charlatans use the illusion to claim superiority over the sore spots they rudely probe in others.

A journalist describing a ball game in a tone of voice suited to a war or Mass.

Sometimes the cat seems not only to be playing with you instead of vice-versa, but to have returned deliberately from the senseless evolutionary 'improvement' of the human cortex. How much net happiness has this organ really contributed?

Call no man a grownup until he is dead, nor woman neither.

In a world with too much knowledge for any one person there will always be a hundred thousand observations that strike us with their originality because we will never encounter the sources they moved five inches away from.

The distribution of guilt is no more rational than the distribution of wealth.

How many geniuses are there who suppressed wonderful insights for the sake of domestic peace or a middling position? How many were seduced into moneymaking? Who starved before creating the theorem that would otherwise inevitably have changed the world?

Because she was continuous he assumed she was integrable but outside the narrow domain they did not converge.

A screenplay compensates some lack. Someone who lived it might not be aware it was missing in other lives.

In past centuries philosophers were persecuted for overturning established ideas and betraying their countrymen; now every nonentity is happy to tell you about the importance of radical novelty and global trade. Nietzsche was far behind our advanced thinkers and publishers, who have since released *Beyond Everything* and a cosmological treatise purporting to describe the ultimate level in cosmic consciousness, *Beyond God*. Our intellectual vanity has kept pace so well with other people's advances in science that before long we must surely see a globe of six billion independent republics, each with its own constitution, central bank, standing army etc.

As soon as he won the lottery he was going to study non-attachment.

Baldly describe your opponent's position as an offshoot of something supposedly discredited.

What the hell is wrong with feeling guilty about making a profit?

To see whether a field is intellectually overripe, examine its political strength among people unequipped to understand it.

The older brain parts have a metaphysical reflex assuring each generation that some shallow formula encompasses all of life.

As usual the examination had nothing to do with the course.

Who wants to bet how many millions of years before Bacon some craftsman insisted only experiment could yield reliable rules? Doubted the parallel postulate?

Charlatans prosper because what people crave is not the truth but the sensation of a vast advance.

The tests of fortune are as good as random. Many of our best-paid citizens would never have been capable of inventing the wheel, or numbers, or the telescope, had they been alive earlier. Many neolithic apemen would be prosperous and well-reputed in the modern economy, using compound interest calculations known to the Mesopotamians.

Flagellating oneself for wrongs done to people who never felt anything but contempt.

A truth planted in a child's mind can crystallize into an absurdity and vice-versa.

Bodybuilders can simply add more weights, but the will comes to a point where its muscles can grow only through sin.

Pluralism and monism fight over whether it is better to express the world in a formula or a series expression. The monist complains that the pluralist is a tourist whose series diverges. The pluralist complains that $1/3$ and $1/15$ are different kinds of things and it is no good saying they "make" $2/5$, which is itself an illegitimate expression really, since 2 is not really divisible by 5.

The pleasure of building a model triumphs over the subject modeled.

Affluence threatens the agenda of unconscious masochism. People want credit for facing this threat.

Vulgar cleverness knows when there is a wider audience for false fifteenth- than for true twentieth-century ideas.

Mathematical similarity between neural clouds of different brains is much the same thing as reincarnation.

Celebrities cater to the public's inchoate desire for regular polyhedrons with ten faces.

A problem preferable to its solution.

A truth like a ladder; writing it down was its use.

Strict application of Occam's razor would have slit the throat of mathematical history by prohibiting substitution of complex expressions for simple ones.

Blessings are uncountable because we know so little about what we have escaped from.

The ratio between two irrational notions can be the same as the ratio between a theorem and an implication.

Old men's voyeurism resembles the pleasure at following solutions to maths problems one no longer cares to solve.

A helpless witness of her own self-destruction.

Vanity would rather be a complex system of epicycles than a mere ellipse.

The importance of culture to humankind. In 47 BC Caesar sets fire to the harbor fleet at Alexandria and burns down the library: 500000 manuscripts. In 392 the Christians destroy the temple of Serapis: another 300000. In 640 the Moslems finish the job. Either the books agree with the Koran and are unnecessary, or they do not and must be destroyed.

Capitalize on the herd's fear of ostracism.

The master wants each slave to regard his colleague as the real oppressor.

Negative numbers started as Hindu debts. A curve with real roots has debt and equity financing; with complex roots, only a business plan.

Genius and progress merge ideas thought disparate and disentangle ideas from corrupt wills. Cardano was first sent to prison for casting the horoscope of Jesus, then hired as the pope's astrologer. Now he would have to pay a dominatrix to lock him up, while the Vatican probably uses the same automated trading software as everyone else to read its tea leaves.

First minimize the hatred of your most powerful enemy.

It is not opposites but incommensurables that attract: a perfect love affair would be a continuing fraction, a repeating decimal with an enormous period.

Ability to recognize and retain ability is useless to a non-employer.

One thing brain research should help with is finding the firing patterns that go with obstructive assumptions like the requirement of constructibility in geometry or heavenly motors in astronomy. Probably there are some ideas that routinely invoke irrelevant emotional areas, and scan like tumors.

Deliberate obscurity is not always charlatanism. Descartes left out some proofs deliberately, to force braggarts into acknowledging his superiority, and Newton was deliberately difficult "to avoid being bated by little smatterers in mathematics".

Power imagines only other people's censorship is an admission of weakness.

They still say God made the world for the sake of human intellect. But only theirs, not their dupes'.

She misrepresented a single coefficient and his dimensionality collapsed.

The new chauvinist pigs. Female chauvinism argues that a physiology specially adapted to the myopic needs of childhood is thereby specially adapted to the management of large industrial nations. Talmudic chauvinism argues that armed disenfranchisement is a victory for equal rights, reason, tolerance.

What sometimes gets us in trouble is imagining we have done nothing new. Newton did not think he had really left Greek geometry behind. Our enemies may know better and hate us for what we did not even know to claim.

The traumatized mind uses obsessive thoughts to buy time against the desperate emergency in the unconscious.

Every widespread innovation feels like the expansion of a simple expression into an elegant series.

How could the preposterous arrogance required to sustain a political campaign coexist with the modesty required toward infinitely complex problems? By chance. Faites vos jeux.

Total lack of preparation can be better than partial, changing a battle to something else.

The noble lie in politics is a divergent series used long enough to obtain a solution. The ignoble lie is the same series used long enough for the next election.

The wise men battling one other over partial differentiation all overlooked their own proximity to the discovery that every function had a trigonometric expansion.

Emotional life is a spherical surface where the angles of a triangle sum to more than 180 degrees; infinite but bounded.

Almost everything said in favor of hunting can be said in favor of gang rape.

Well-crafted secondary characters are involutes of the main action.

In judging others we project their surfaces onto planes with too few or too many dimensions. Their space curves unfairly reduce to lines or swell to hyper-objects. Our non-conformal maps fail to conserve angles properly. Or we insist on particular rather than generalized coordinates.

Political pluralism falsely denies it possible that a unified physical theory could ever come to embrace human brains. Political monism falsely asserts such a theory is already in principle available.

If Nature does nothing superfluous she must lack humor.

In a population explosion the capitalist asceticism of thrift serves only to finance an ever-increasing number of people forced into the capitalist asceticism of thrift.

Whatever his initial intentions, the junkie renounces the world more thoroughly than the priest once he dispenses with clean reputation and good works.

Personality has rational coefficients but talent is transcendental.

Probably the twenty varieties of sperm competing in the vagina of a lioness all think they are soldiers of Moral Rearmament or Humanitarian Invasion.

Idealistic young people think that with enough good will a positive integral solution can be found to every problem.

A good schoolmaster will fill young people with fearful awareness of the insane flood of publications.

She did not understand why the odds of her infidelity dampened their ardor. Why was their brain not excommunicated?

A skilled politician knows which vulgar contradictions can successfully be revealed as hidden unities. Your sensational revelations that Negroes too breathe air, that women like good pay, earn you the admiration appropriate to discovering algebraic functions can be represented transcendentally.

The correlation between self-esteem and merit is random.

The best literature states the insoluble differential equations of a psychological system.

Each generation thinks all continents of the intellectual world have been discovered and only some mapping remains. If intellectual space is spherical, some generation will eventually be right about this.

For every object no matter how beautiful or large there exists some angle from which it can be forced to yield a tiny, ugly shadow.

The devil likes to make us choose between feeling useless for doing nothing and feeling stupid for doing something unacceptable.

Happy couples are vector products, unhappy scalar.

Liken your opponent's authorities to the longstanding errors of antiquity.

Other people's political murders originate in flimsy utopian illusion.

A corporation is a modulus system, limited numbers of roles spiraling.

How many leading women have slept with only one influential man?

Youth can scarcely anticipate the vehement hatred awaiting any proof it is intelligent enough to sense the blind egotism of established wills.

In love at first sight you sense a whole family of invariants you would otherwise have to interpolate from statistics.

Avoid argument with people known for low blows.

Nature keeps asking us 'why'? like a little girl until we ask her to shut up.

Any level of accomplishment that seems to give perfect satisfaction is an infinity, but there is always another level of infinity beyond. You play Chopin and make yourself cry, then you hear someone else playing it right, eyes dry.

If metaphysics is really so misleading nonsense phrases may be the deepest meditations after all, their phonology lighting up random outliers on the conceptual spectrum.

Your neighbor wastes his resources; if you stole them you would do much better.

Hack writing is scalar, mediocrity vector, genius tensor, transformable into any cultural coordinates and back out again, perhaps not preserving absolute distances but watertight in the relations of its partial derivatives.

Each society's males despised the other's for failing to exaggerate their masculinity.

Paranoia introduces an occult force of gravity to account for the curvature of mental space.

Youth is not sufficiently warned against the invisible wounds that leave the cortex at the mercy of the reptilian core.

They bankrolled one character trait only to find they had fattened it up for another.

Fate is spiteful and loves to place us at humiliating disadvantage to what we thought was negligible, but there is a kind of jiujitsu that turns this to advantage, however unconsciously. We sometimes obtain occult help by denying the usefulness of something virtuous, as Einstein denied the usefulness and even the good faith of higher-mathematical exposition in natural philosophy, prompting fate to spite him into eternal fame by sending him Riemannian geometry and tensor analysis.

Moral death precedes physical by decades.

Every increase in worldliness has something in common with the realization that operations like addition and subtraction are merely special cases of a more abstract algebra.

Our internal angel grows bored with us and deserts us, leaving thoughts from outside proliferating like raging weeds.

If the history of sex is anything to go by, the strictness of sanctions increases directly with the universality and intensity of desire. Taboos on suicide must be fighting a practically universal longing; but the skin trade is growing so fast that the air must be going out of the sex tires.

One is meant not to fear for the morrow but the core Christian sentiment is really "Eli, lama sabachthani", which the psychiatrists used to call basic anxiety. No wonder so many prefer cheery guilt.

The reason great wits are oft to madness near allied is that space is curved in both their worlds. The curvature is different but you can still perceive the similarity between the left hand and the right.

Beg the question of whether your examples really add up to your general principle.

No education is strong enough to prevent internalizing at least part of some invincible injustice.

Russell's Spanish nurse said half the friendships in the world would dissolve instantly if all were known; how many of the dissolutions would be suicides?

By the time the knife was sharp enough to cut there was no meat.

Some defeats put the world behind glass and destroy confidence in the possibility it might be worth breaking.

Moldy lemons make moldy lemonade.

Never trust anyone too obviously accomplished at his own profit.

Governments argue that habitual drug users are addicts. Since they are not acting voluntarily, their money should be confiscated. This sophistry is less obviously predatory than a tax on wheelchair access or yellow skin.

A pity that the ability instantly to recognize the morbidity of an emotional state when it hits others has so little to do with the ability ever to remove it from ourselves.

What sort of person dreams up a God with nothing better to do than humiliate his creatures?

Force of will exponentiates impotence into nilpotency.

Mental atrophy gives us more empathy for amputees and cripples.

Too late they discovered that they had enlisted one another in a game of 'too late'.

In the book of life we will find out how many abused children profited from their premature loss of illusions.

Much hatred of erotica is really a wish to extract more resources from the desires of the opposite sex. The skin traders outrage their competitors by offering 51% of the pleasure for 1% of the price. The retaliation: a race to the bottom where no one's attentions are worth a penny but everyone remains saddled with the desire for affections that are.

Why would the cause of a destroyed identity be more obvious than a blocked vein leading to a heart attack?

Siphoning energy away from neurotic defensiveness presumes there will be a market for it elsewhere. But what if the neurotics gang up on the liberated person?

It is too easy to slip from the falsification of theories into the falsification of other people.

She had no problem being seen as a lust object but was humiliated when they reduced her to a sales prospect.

Points of corruption force us to draw a different personality curve, but because we are always forced to interpolate points from our own motives and character it is not really fair to charge us with naivete if the curve has to be reshaped again and again for fresh crimes.

She was infuriated, and later scornful, about his placid help in organizing her infidelities; it was too obvious he had quickly written her off as a whore; the fool deserved to be proven right. In reality his dull detachment was a fraud, forced upon him by his role; he was the only person who would ever understand a certain thing about her; her blindness was terribly hurtful; but the persona at least saved him from sharing the dishonor she carelessly heaped upon it; and sadly she was in fact a whore.

An attic of a mind, crammed with beautiful things in a state of dry rot.

The American lady, a corporate lawyer, said disdainfully to an admirer of Thomas Jefferson: "but he died in debt." The founder was not up to her standards, not conservative enough for a graduate of Ivy Law Academy. He did not collect enough rents or usury to rank in the glorious company of those who understand money is wealth. He borrowed where better, deader men had the sense to sell worthless shares. If his ideas had been worth anything his fellow slave-holders would have ensured he died rich, like Mozart and Euler. His books would still be on the New York newspapers' bestseller lists, not moldering on some forgotten shelf. She took her listeners' silence as proof of her annihilating brilliance. Money is truth, and truth money; that was all she knew, and all she needed to know. She had more of it than Jefferson because she was a superior soul.

No ruler in the next century will be worthy of the name without a mathematics tutor. It is no longer appropriate for a sovereign to be an idiot in the study of forms.

If the brain were the true organ of sex as sometimes maintained one would expect a great many more doddering husbands.

Suicide is likely to trigger hate in some quarters and grief in others and we have a duty to ensure one does not seize on the other unless they both want it to, unless there are masochistic motives hidden in someone who might regret our death.

Vulgarity regards all getting as earning, hence all redistribution as theft, vandalism, parasitism. Others may receive the tools of their trade from the Divinity and the intellectual demigods of the past; vulgarity creates them all itself ex nihilo, along with the infrastructure that sustains and transports its customers.

Their conversation demonstrated the existence of a solution but they could not integrate.

Beliefs like diseases eluding medicine behind the blood-brain barrier. Kronecker had no problem denying the existence of irrational numbers.

Resentment at being passed over for someone whose ignorance merely has a different shape. Is not ours just as infinite?

The most important truths cannot be proved in a finite number of steps.

Fortunate whose strivings are blocked only by circumstance.

"Welfare reform" is American for "Arbeit macht frei".

Major crises in life push us from the fertile errors of analysis into the desert of foundations.

If you advance routine Christian ideas about money you will be thought to have made them up yourself in an irresponsible protest against the treadmill of 'growth'. Society also insists Karl Marx was not in a position to judge Judah.

Mankind is divided into the camps of those who are and are not satisfied by the demonstration that the opposite of a thing is a contradiction.

Christian theocracy is so fraudulent that it cannot claim clear title even to Narnia. In the Tark Shastra, Nirnéya means immediate arrival at truth; Bábá Nânac used the names Nárnján and Naráyana for God, since Nārāyana is supreme Vishnu, the Ancient Man whose abode was once the endless waters. In his four hands he holds the conch, the discus, the mace, and the lotus; on his breast is the divine Kaustabha jewel distilled from the ambrosia which he alone could give the lesser gods the stamina to stir from the ocean's womb using the titanic Magic Mountain as a ladle. When it comes time to steal the ambrosia back from the daemons, he incarnates himself not as the King of Beasts -- hero, conqueror and cuckold -- but as the infinitely voluptuous Mohinī, the more powerful of the two great levers that move the world.

In school we learn reductio ad absurdum but not how little evil people care about their absurdity.

Deny to the last that your king is dead.

You can receive truth from outside but typically it comes like nicotine in cigarette smoke, mixed with endless irrelevant chemicals. Your mind hardens to them the way the lungs do smoke, and withdrawal has the same hazards.

There must be some self whose fate does not enjoy spiting resolutions, undermining moral undertakings, rendering renunciations vain, denying actions reinforcing fruit, or posing them against some more powerful agenda.

Repressing hatred just accumulates interest for an inconvenient deadline. Expressing hatred just entangles you in retaliation. Time to go for a long run.

In sex education they do not tell you about the day of complete disillusionment, when you might be content to shut down hormone production altogether were it not for the side effects.

The body has its own nobility which says no to particularly monstrous infidelities.

External evils that thwart us too completely produce evil thoughts the same way the stomach produces excess acid during an involuntary fast.

Vain people may hallucinate most of their virtues and talents but at least they nourish their good ones.

No danger of her suffocating herself with excessive regard for the great minds of the past!

Disinheritance kills.

The fragments game reminds you of the bitterest defeats and the happiest victories but also of a thousand situations you will never have the chance to test.

Sin multiplies like success, it is success in undermining our better side.

A politician whose moral stature varied inversely with his enthusiasm for robbing citizens of redress.

When no other objection is available, argue the weakness of human knowledge.

The deadly sins have all been exposed as harmless garter snakes. Anger and envy are constructive against tractable evils; pride can be more constructive than depression, sloth than industrious vice, gluttony and covetise than a sluggish economy; lust with antibiotics and contraceptives is good exercise; avarice distracts old people from the rancid fun of spoiling youth's pleasures. So what seems missing from people with no sense of sin? It is as if excessive integration with their circumstances has submerged them at the end of their character arc.

People complacent about the infidelities of their spouses strike us as having themselves lied at the altar.

Looking vainly among the enemies of one's friends for a parallel to arouse interest in a type of injustice which has frustrated all effort at redress.

Who got the clever idea of convincing people virtue consisted in going without, forever?

When we are out of our element long enough the mind reduces its investment in consciousness.

Anomie culminates in the zombie, spiritually oxidized by banality, tethered to the world only by the ludicrous persistence of the organism, beneath rather than outside time. His ideals, projects, acquaintances, courtesy, sexual viability, his grounds for all these things, go on spinning, but pointlessly, like a detached flywheel on a broken motor. If he feeds the hungry they will make ten more starving brats. If he increases the efficiency of computers he will merely address the ghostly desires of ghostly personalities. He is a weightlifter condemned to a room with no choices other than 5-pound dumbbells and 1200-pound squats: he can either wiggle his arms for a million repetitions, gaining no muscle, or do the squats and break his spine. This ought to be depressing but instead there is the fizz of an empty Nirvana. Active people including unwitting zombies despise the zombie because they do not grasp the conditions that snuffed him out.

Empty compartments in our lives cause vacuums and break down useful firewalls.

There are still a handful of tribes that have never seen a white man, and undersea animals no white man has seen, but the Mystic East has melted even faster than the glaciers. If you were to see a Tibetan magician walking naked through the winter winds of a hidden valley at one hundred miles per hour, exuding blue light from a parallel cosmos, he would nonetheless be fiddling with a music player, or trying to send a milnet note about an unnecessary meeting, or grant solicitation, or television contract, or tax dodge. There is nowhere for a fragrant Orientalism to hide once the labor-saving scientists split the atom of banality and pusillanimity: within a month every organism on the planet harbors at least one of the toxic waste particles; the metaphysical frontier is closed, to us and to the Orientals who would flee into Occidentalism. Even physical travel becomes a self-indulgent anachronism, an obsolete reflex like the hatred which survives the antagonist's death. The illusion of a suitably daemonic enemy collapses when the wicked Iranian sorcerer in his far-off lair is exposed as just one more dissatisfied electronics customer, transforming his ephemeral impulses into a permanent chemical stain on the data landscape.

Find an example of a ridiculous or dangerous person who agrees with your enemy.

A geriatric home for rebels.

A great aphorism is an analytic expression equivalent to a convergent infinite series containing great novels recursively containing great aphorisms.

Never harbor the friends or relations of people you have killed.

Fanatics expecting us to admire their firm beliefs are Calibans expecting a lady to melt at the sight of their pimpled erections. The strange thing is that in the voting booth she really does melt.

Dramatically execute the person you have hired to do your dirty work.

Improvements in brain scans revealed that the adherents of a 9th century Zoroastrian sect must have received 99% of the philosophy extractable from vector analysis. For a firm intuitive grasp of quantum physics you had to have been a housewife in the first Chinese empire.

Consciousness is so inconstant that every day amounts to a thousand transmigrations.

Did Aquinas realize that he had stolen the ontological argument from the Magists? Do his successors realize that the angels watching over them are Persian?

If poets and philosophers are linguistic musicians, demagogues are fakirs fascinated by the snake.

The ability to desaturate neuronal associations is the fountain of youth.

Quaintnesses differ as much as their namesake.

Privacy invasion is doubly unjust when the victim's consciousness of it degrades his personality into preoccupation with potentially humiliating trivialities.

Ask too many questions for your opponent to have time for refutation.

Many assume they have standing to participate in a cultural war worthy of the name.

The claim that a finite mind can mirror an infinite being is the most successful fraud in history. The second most successful is the claim that one finite mind can mirror an arbitrarily large collection of other finite minds.

Nothing is exotic in a perfect market.

Make your enemy think his opinions will cost him money.

Paralyzed by the Medusan spectacle of vileness at the helm.

The weapons created employment for people who needed never have existed.

An intellectual arsonist who prides himself on his gold matchbook and the scale of his forest fires.

Knowing how to find cavities and plunge in the drill, he wanted a diploma in dentistry.

Shuffle the order of your questions to conceal their overall thrust.

Reincarnation was a succession of long marriages, each ending in drawn-out emotional bankruptcy, with vice drawing her further and further from the fountain of youth.

Internal anxiety is as real and unreal as external malice.

The longest list of zeros that ever followed a one; the longest headstand ever performed; holding one's breath for three days; walking on water to fetch cigarettes from the store; resurrection in the form of a squirrel.

Burnout is the morbid cousin of nirvana: when desire is thoroughly exhausted one is almost as well off as one would have been after satisfaction and disillusionment. By the time the rescuers arrive one would almost be content to remain stranded.

Asceticism is a nuclear attack on the logical contradictions implicit in our desires.

Murderers sincerely offended at lack of appreciation for their art form. Is it really necessary to go on about the victims, who have after all left suffering behind? What about the cleverness of the strategy, and the handsome compound interest reaped from the booty?

People quarrel over nonsense because their opponents are denying the evolutionary validity of the intuitive pictures underlying their axioms.

Reason vainly scolds as everyone rushes to satisfy passion. Perhaps if children were taught to sell everything their rebellion would show whether anything really exists outside the cash nexus.

In transmigration too every soul rises to its level of incompetence – perhaps even the Deity.

Ascetics boast that liberation from the tyranny of concupiscence has elevated them into a realm of beautiful nymphs and roses.

The best way to destroy someone is to trick him into a habit that contradicts his self-image; existence becomes chronic remorse.

She collected experiences at a frantic pace, not realizing her mental legs would eventually buckle under the weight of ineffaceable memory.

Will there be a refund desk at the Resurrection of the Body for when they find out that only the closed-form expression has been resurrected?

At first the idea went away when he told it to. One day it sneeringly announced that it was claiming title to his mind under the doctrine of adverse possession. Earlier it had merely wounded other ideas; now it wanted them extinct. -- The demons of sense are weaklings by comparison with a negative intellectual fascination churning the processor of consciousness.

Someone capable of forming opinions can easily forget how much envy he can arouse in people accustomed to buy theirs at oligopoly prices.

Her seemingly erratic moods were actually in perfect synch with Saturn.

Genetic engineering returns us full circle to the eagle heads and dragon tails of the ancient gods.

In a world ruled by evil, parenthood is a sin and abortion a kindness. Someone who asserts the contrary has reason to believe rational parents would not want them.

Happiness at the survival of youthful desire forgets the fate of the glutton, who has also managed to pry the governor off the engine.

To be a Yezdanian and worship the stars we would have to forget that a tiny mind does not really know what aspect of things to worship. To the gods we must seem like the flatterer who seeks our favor by praising our most distasteful relative.

He thought her ambition to eject him from paradise had to be just bored goodness striking a flirtatious evil pose.

Long books explain that if you dig up all the minerals in a mountain you flatten the landscape and poison the streams.

How much squandering of public resources stems from female voters' misplaced assumption that everything you bleed away will be back next month?

How many competitors do you need in ultra-high-technology markets before the duplication of efforts causes greater inefficiencies than totalitarian bureaucracy? What experiment could ever be devised to find out?

Outright imitation of Versailles is intellectually superior to half-baked architectural allusion.

While conceding that almost all improvements in his industry traced back to social activists rather than businessmen, the good professor insisted that because the public interest is occasionally served by entrepreneurial self-interest it is always served by entrepreneurial self-interest. We sipped our wine and toasted the new era of wise environmental stewardship. Behind us on the viewing screen a Khazar bomb blew apart the twentieth Semite child of the day; the yahoo commentator congratulated himself on chronicling this blow against "anti-Semitic terrorism".

Ninety-five percent of politics is nothing more than the criminal's jeer: "So what are you going to do about it, sucker?"

The lady resented the indecent implication that she had created a larger mountain of indissoluble trash than had other species. Her boyfriend gallantly finessed her error, explaining that what really galled her was the way the liberals denied their own complicity in the mess. -- Three years later the federal authorities arrested him for buying erotic images of children.

Cowards had better silence and slander their victims.

When an author begins by acknowledging a thousand people he is calling in IOUs rather than paying them off. The tribe's collective capital is being summoned as security for a loan. With that many predecessors, might the book as a whole not already have effectively been written? Better an author whose isolation suggests he might have stumbled across a raw diamond.

What does society gain from proofs that a false leader possesses the sickly strength to break china?

Represent mob support as proof of overwhelming logic.

The very last drop of water will still sell for a penny if no one can face the fact that it is the last.

Some politicians fall in love with external costs the same way perverts fall in love with knickers: the sight of the poisoned stream reminds them of the money that brought their baubles.

A coral reef was destroyed because a gilded redneck wanted to see his face on a television screen.

We mock those who deny the sphericity of the earth but not those who deny its finitude.

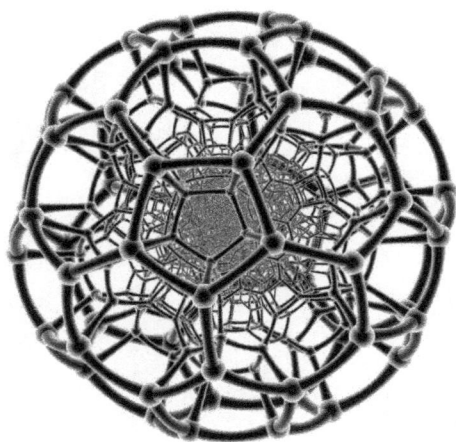

She explained that her delicate condition resulted from an 'imbalance' in chemicals which she could scarcely name, and not only she: no two neurologists could agree on them either without the help of a salesman. She was unbalanced because she was not in balance.

They deny evolution but assume our bodies will instantly adopt to a world without air or water -- by the will of the Divinity, whom they thereby paint as so capricious that he might as well be called Chance.

Why should someone for whom even human art is too subversive be equipped to understand the Divinity's art?

Use of words like 'democracy' and 'Christianity' may be a symptom of Reverse Tourette's Syndrome, blurted out in mid-sublimation of some unspeakable sex act.

Aging is the scar of evil passions. Love rejuvenates not only through pleasure but by restoring equanimity in the face of intractable evil.

Postponing acknowledgement of Malthus has been one of humanity's most expensive projects. "Perhaps if we squeeze more use out of each product we will stop breeding beyond available goods."

It flattered his intellectual vanity that he had swindled the workers into paying so much interest to make up for his reduced taxes. Clearly he was at least twenty percent cleverer than the stupid.

If murder were taxable there would be no national debt.

Unusual, certainly, but would it be cruel to put war criminals to work fishing aluminum tins and steel plates out of landfills and automobile graveyards? Would it not be less cruel in the long run than having the chain gangs pave new roads whose cars will ultimately asphyxiate everyone? What a jaunty figure certain deskbound warriors would cut in their striped suits and caps, manfully rummaging through rotten bananas and cat litter to bring society metals unstained by conflict. Reclaiming wasted calories, they would even spare us the expense of a prison mess hall.

Begin your proofs with the enemy's most cherished lies.

Brilliant economy created a vehicle that weighed scarcely more than a man and went a million miles between charges. The customers rejected it because only a ten-ton tank could begin to calm their projected fear that others were about to preempt their plan to steal all the oil in the world to fill their ten-ton tanks.

She was so yesterday's rent-seeker.

The modern grandee has a pitiable responsibility for ever-increasing hordes dependent on obsolescent modes of production.

Pro-life Christianity is a popular American contradiction in terms. Christ was militantly anti-life: childless, motherless, poor, suicidal, a mocker, a whiner, a quitter with no office, no promotion, no property, no connections, no capital gain. A loser, a flash in the pan, a charlatan, a weakling. An anti-American a[ ]e. His ideas are represented in the United States by a small faction of left-wing Jews.

To maximize the gross national product the Security Council decreed every citizen should receive angioplasty.

Unbeknownst to either, the dead author had lived solely to delight the jobless professor.

Imitating the low-energy, non-toxic production of the placid beasts freed up an enormous amount of fresh capital for instruments of mass murder.

Propaganda puts grooves in our brains because it is combatting the life-lies other organisms need to repeat incessantly.

Each despised the other for taking fifty years to discover what he had seen immediately.

He shuddered with revulsion as he watched her wholehearted self-approbation at a line she had stolen from him; but would it have come into existence had she not needed it, and without her admirers would there have been anyone left to appreciate it?

An egoless person without any tic intense enough to metamorphose into scholarly expertise.

She was pleased with herself for her resolution in resisting an inconvenient importunity. The flower was only pretending to need water.

People who condemn living in books do not know how lucky one is to share a man's conversation without risking a share in the energy hemorrhage of his circumstances.

He insisted that his murders were a political revolution, as the survivors would have more goods per capita.

We were supposed to enjoy the productive assets while the proles were taught narcissistic identification with the fake nationalism of increasingly foreign-owned enterprises. But as we sell all the productive assets we ourselves become narcissistic proles.

Vampire without a cause. By finally resigning him to endless disruption her incessant demands ended up stealing his soul, which she did not really know what to do with.

A vice is a tyrannical cabal of brain cells exploiting some miserable lower organ.

Journalism has the unfair advantage that we are at times obliged to monitor the emergencies which might destroy our opportunities for interests beyond the journalistic.

Academic degrees are cash receipts.

Killing on the off chance. -- A ladybug crossed the desk just as he was leaving. It would surely never return and its chemistry was unlikely to stain anything but he killed it on the off chance. -- A strange bird was hovering around the crops. Its appetite did not seem whetted but he killed it on the off chance. -- Has there ever really existed anyone stupid enough to believe the divine mind wants them to throw rocks at a stranger? Has there ever really existed anyone else?

Never acquire anything you cannot afford to defend.

His political thesis was remarkably free of intellectual poison. He had siphoned the reek of the stadium lavatory from public affairs until his book resembled the tempeh Japanese scientists extract from sewage. The reactionaries missed the gaminess of the dead blood cells and despised him as an insipid weakling.

Indirect or flimsy answers hint at a weak spot. Is it a weakness in your opponent's argument, or are you just cruelly reminding him of some grief?

The autocratic executive donned latex wings to play his mistress' worker bee.

A vehicle that only ran on vinegar: the brilliance she displayed in parochial subjects turned out to be unavailable for any theme too abstract to stimulate Gland M.

The lady moose never let him forget she was an authentic member of the deer family.

As he lay there stuck and dejected the villains thought they were about to cull a sickly victim. But he had merely stumbled across a trap laid by a long-forgotten furrier, and needed not move to do them in.

To gain feminine respect and be counted a sincere admirer of JS Mill you were to castrate yourself and vow perpetual relative poverty, permanently forfeiting feminine respect.

People who make killings in the market cause the same problems as elephant hunters in Africa: the prey runs out and the tusks do not really cure impotence.

He wanted moral credit for putting her out of the misery he had caused her.

Average alpha and would-be alpha males live on the border of diminishing returns, given the bureaucratic overhead of dominating the pack, the exponentially increasing existential insurance premiums. The glands often recognize the checkmate and scale back or shut down testosterone production, but the brain rarely sees the trap closing; if it did, the artists and scientists might lose their position as unacknowledged legislators.

The two different varieties of pacifist went at each other like doves in nature until their feathers were gone and their skin dripping red.

When someone says it is the principle of the thing he usually means the principle comfortable to his irrationality.

It is a mistake to imagine the corporate media too full of lies for anyone to obtain an accurate sketch of events. A good hunter can read amazing things from a tiny heap of scat.

Politics is reducing all others to dreams by reducing oneself to nightmare.

Get your enemy to agree to some truth, then baldly assert it has something to do with your case.

In a new Depression one of the functions of a renewed civilian corps could be a revival of the calendar ethos shared by the ancient Mayans and Persians, with a different angel ruling each day of the month: 365 varieties of symbolic unity per year.

It was not the devil but God who gave men the chemical knowledge to avoid the grossest form of reincarnation. The devil enjoys watching fools in labor queues. He laughs as each mother scratches her head at the failure of her plan to be reborn as the only one snapping up marginal productivity increases.

The eccentric cousin of a perfectly reasonable proposition.

Rogues imagine they can pick and choose whose interests will be regarded as illusory.

If genetic engineers produced soldiers like Mithra, with ten thousand eyes and a thousand ears, would they be selected for, or would they have the same reproductive struggles as incomprehensible genius?

Between him and success stood a single misfiring neuron.

Thus actually spake Zarathustra: if you want to get into Paradise, be sure to hide your used toothpicks in a wall. Do not pour water out at night, particularly towards the East. If you are on the rag, do not look at the stars or the fire. Kill as many frogs as you can because they are aggressors. Begin each day by rubbing your hands with cow's urine. Never pee standing up or without repeating the Avesta etc. at least ten times. Never put off 'til tomorrow what you can do today.

The Almighty begins our mental journey with both vivid mirages and real oases, then strips them both away until we have a single camel, a water bottle, endless sands and a profusion of dream images so pale and ephemeral they can no longer tempt us out of our way. We wonder why He does not reverse the arrow of time.

A satanic refinement of evolution had given the mendacious murderers the ability to induce so self-destructive a degree of exasperation in their betters that they insisted their marvelous predominance had to be the work of a god rather than a random mutation.

Education absurdly assumes that you can become better and better at speaking the truth without moving further and further away from the interests of self-deceivers and liars.

The Hebrew god heeded their prayer that in the wilderness waters would break out, and streams in the desert; but to do it he melted the polar ice caps. Might they not have achieved the same result by praying to Satan?

The reason Einstein smelled a rat in the continuous spectrum of quantum energy concentration probabilities is that the zillion potential states of a particle are more like the millions of distinct hypotenuses possessed by the most humble high-dimensional triangle. Fiendishly clever statistics are an odd path to the hypotenuse of a triangle, though you may get useful results for a while as you do from many fallacies.

Prove your opponent's authorities contradict him elsewhere.

If you pretend that finite and culturally conditioned superiorities entitle you to the infinite superiority of the live murderer over the dead victim, by the time the mistake becomes obvious you may well have clear title to a solid gold palace.

A culture is a probability distribution of hormonal stimulants. Related cultures differ in their exponents rather than the underlying distribution.

Feign the modesty of an intelligence too great to venture opinions in the hazardous arena chosen by your frivolous, reckless opponent.

There can be more dissonance in two identical waves subtly out of phase than in wildly different waves.

The rise of electronic culture is the rise of 51% stimuli. Easier to get by with no love if you at least have more than half the sex chatter. Which selects against love.

When the average person talks about genes refining themselves over a million generations of environmental challenge, what if anything is going on in his mind that would not be going on were he discussing reincarnation? Is there any cross-section of the material world that cannot be construed as a gene machine, and might it not be that the successful conclusion of all genetic adaptation is a transmutation into the wholly inorganic, the celestial, eliminating the diminishing returns inevitable in the fraudulent rewards of biologically-rooted consciousness? Do you win Vishnu's simulation game by leaving it?

Alienation has its Riemann surfaces where characters play branch cuts between intersecting sheets. From a bed in a motel room you pass via the taxi cut to a state funeral. All part of a single-valued function where your identity is the unknown.

Gods ejected from paradise are not always guilty of devouring their karmic capital. The Divinity of Divinities may not play dice with the universe but he does play cards, and if he did not shuffle the deck now and then he would forever be playing the same hand.

Divinity is by any definition a function of more than diurnal dimensionality and consequently multivalent. Messiahs by the boatload, self-replicating fractals.

The tortoise avatar Cancer dubbed himself a crab, to inspire fear of his claws.

Failure: a paradoxical or indeterminate expansion of a reasonable function into $\{-1/2 = 1-1+1-1+1...\}$

The devil is doubly amused if he can ensnare us in addiction to the magical devices that helped us escape his snares.

Every organism and every cross-section of every ecosphere is a time-series prediction engine.

The sines of a spherical love triangle can add up to three.

The diabetics demanded that everyone be subject to daily insulin injections. "Besides, it will create jobs".

The Christian version of Lucifer's fall neglects to mention the ambitions of his wife; the Persians do not make this mistake.

If you travel two miles, take a right-angle left turn and travel another 2j miles, you have traveled 2+2j miles without retracing your steps or moving in a circle, yet you are back where you started. If you travel backwards n miles, take a right-angle right turn and travel another nj miles, you have traveled n+nj miles in a different pattern, without retracing your steps or moving in a circle, yet you are back where you started. If you do not make your turns at right angles, then instead of ending up back where you started, you end up at a point whose distance from your starting point has more than one value, though all the values are square roots of the same complex number. -- In a more than one-dimensional world even the most primitive of determinists is already so far down the rabbit hole that only fools insist the single Riemann surface of the organism we see during the day is somehow existentially richer than the neural backwash we swim through in dreamtime.

Religion distrusts the imagination because so many of its seemingly regular curves end up verging into squiggles. But some chaotic graphs have pristine, even trivial analytic expressions.

Be patiently bewildered by your enemy's irritation at your incessant question-begging.

Mothers reasonably enough regard their offspring as religious symbols beyond the capacity of any artist who has yet lived; but the same reasoning justifies doting on pets, on plants, on whores. Like most enemies, pantheistic nature mysticism and deism are asymptotes, since nature is the most complex symbol of Deity we could ever hope to find, and the rest is unknowable anyway.

Sneering injustice loves to contemplate its grandeur in the smashed mirror of the minds it has poisoned. So few people are naturally immune to this poison that even Christ and Buddha could not always maintain the Hindu perfection of restraint in cursing evildoers.

Sometimes when the body awakens too early we later learn it has clumsily anticipated some pending event. It knows it has found an appropriate use for our emergency time reserves, but does not always know how to make the nature of the use conscious, so we waste the precious time reading drivel, encounter the disaster we had a last-minute chance to avoid, and lose sleep into the bargain.

In the hours before dawn the secret legislators and their acolytes return to life. No one is ringing to swindle you into overcrowded vacation property or penny stocks or penis enlargement pills. There are no engines roaring to interrupt the playing of Maurice Ravel. The ghostly imam lights a hashish pipe and opens pages uncut for a hundred years, and no brute bursts in to denounce him as a terrorist and drag you off to prison.

Any God worth worshipping would regard the homages and offerings of its simulated beings with even more contempt than we regard the half-eaten birds and rodents our cats sometimes decide to grace us with. "Thinkest thou that I will eat human flesh, and drink the blood of Arabs?" It might enjoy watching us doing equations or playing instruments or scribbling false metaphysics, as we enjoy watching our cats with a piece of yarn.

Unattainable virtue wounds self-esteem more than indefensible vice.

Pornography recycles the Tantric wish to live in the queen's bhaga. Some of the ancient Hindus dispensed with even more sublimations, handing over their wives to their gurus and making wife-swapping at the cannibal graveside a regular communion, singing ritual songs at climax. In Kashmir, where the Durds were wont to sell their houses complete with both wife and children, the city of Kashial had the world's merriest widows; if there was no son, male visitors were expected to offer condolences sincere enough to guarantee the bereaved lady the joy of an heir.

When everything is accessible electronically, the only real pilgrimages remaining will be abstract.

The Hindus describe sensual reality as a malady because three real dimensions are a perceptual prison.

An American brain surgeon once said that because of his high fees he had seen more than his share of paradises, but that the fool's paradise trumped them all. A zero-overhead perpetuum mobile. Can it be that the idiot who gives his money and his wife away to his guru has stumbled across the neural state of which all the others are wannabe shears and translations? What difference does it make whether pleasures cloy or not, if you get infinite pleasure from indifference to all pleasure?

The janitor's god uses a silver dustpan and a golden brush.

Correct to six decimal places reviles correct to two thousand. "I can be mechanically implemented but you cannot."

All gratifications resemble opium. Once familiarity makes the brain contemptuous of the stimulus, you need more and more until one day you notice you have time for little else. Ascetic mastery springs the trap of pleasure, dabbles in opium all its life without the body forming a habit that will force consciousness to go cold turkey in the shocking event that it survives its physical avatar.

The detachment that renders the earth pure silver, or the disdain which is the treasurer of hell.

The Muslims say God created the souls four thousand years before he created the bodies. A software engineer who wrote the code engine and later tacked on the cosmetic front end.

The East has wearied of the Prophet's insistence that hope is as brutish as fear, both being figments of the deceitful, feminine imagination. The West has wearied of the scientists' insistence that there might be technological hope without catastrophic side-effects. So our blue-haired matrons do yoga and theirs have love affairs, and every meadow is ruined with a fake palace.

The Bodhisattva has woven a mental fabric which the brutishness of worldly affairs cannot stain. The rest of us have to make do with stuff that repels coffee stains, or wine, or dirt, but never all of them, nor even the one we need.

Psychopaths are morally tone-deaf. They know the emotional phrase by heart but may or may not understand the individual words, or understand that they are separate words, or that they were orchestrated for strings rather than horns, for baritone rather than tenor.

Silkworms may be more useful than butterflies, but the Fable of the Bees works better if the useful agents of corruption are exterminated as they ripen into murderers.

To illustrate the wondrous efficiencies of private enterprise and the free market, a secret government committee removed all military responsibilities from the Defense Department and reassigned them at ten times the cost to mercenaries exempt from auditing and murder investigation.

"Free market" is American for "corporate state".

Their first step in universalizing American democracy was to abolish democratic checks and balances outside America; the second step was to abolish them within America.

The Jewish State was such a success that they founded a Druid State.

Yahoos think the command of the army is a license to declare war. What is the point of having power if you have to have good reason for starting a brawl? Hell, what would life be without the spice of murder? Did any great man ever dispense with murder? And if murder has always existed, is the criminal law really anything more than a childish fantasy? Who needs a justice system when you can have "political energy"? – These doctrines were preached at Cambridge until the undergraduates began to find them a poor excuse for an unprecedented personal and national debt and, taking their deep-fried Thrasymachus at his word, strung him up by the balls in Harvard Yard.

Nietzsche had drafted a current-affairs sequel, "Beneath Good and Evil", but his sister locked him up and stole his manuscript, so he had to recite the work in grunts and screams from his upstairs bedroom during her piano soirées.

The fun of an exotic algebra too easily washes away the desire to model reality.

Carbon deposits had clogged three quarters of his mental fuel injectors.

Brazilian bikini waxes betray unconscious pedophilia, and "Schamhaare" is not always a misnomer, but truth in advertising makes as much sense here as anywhere else. Better to know up front: "Property of the State of California. Penalty for failure to rinse: $100".

From the necessity for world government they deduced the inevitability of their own imperial grandeur, modeled on the comic books of their childhoods.

Lazy intellectual egotism prefers the title Staunch Faith.

The evangelist faulted his atheist friend for undue cynicism about religious institutions, but they kissed and made up, able to agree heartily that race murder in the service of trade is no vice. Together these moral demigods and their political friends had forced vast hordes of exiles to spend their working hours sucking fat businessmen's pricks. So did Christ die in vain or not?

Both the civilized and the barbaric want each other's moral credit for free, but a verbose bodybuilder is a lesser evil than a bloodthirsty lawmaker.

Probabilistic laws of nature are a religious halfway-house between two deterministic eras.

She could drive a thousand miles per gallon of emotional fuel.

A god who instructs souls to learn from suffering is putting rats in a maze.

Why would the satisfaction of spiritual achievement be any less fleeting than any other satisfaction? Because it alters the basic mechanism of perception? How do you judge which such alterations constitute progress and which delusion?

The religion of art is the tribute virtue pays to vice.

The bizarre excesses of certain yogis who view everything as the same level of illusion amount to a confusion between different species of transfinite numbers.

Which health statistics can honestly claim to have discounted correctly for the somatic impact of usury?

An alien philosopher with time on his hands might wonder, as some of us do about the beasts, whether we qualify as ensouled. His comrades might mock him as a sentimental pedant, or denounce him as a terrorist crackpot undermining crucial research on a cure for alien gout.

Parents who worry that erotica will spoil their children for really existing personal life should worry much more about exposing them to the grand masters in poetry and philosophy, who can make reality look more insipid than a watered-down drink; not to mention the sages, who pity you for bothering with the cosmos at all.

People who misunderstand us factorize us wrongly. They rudely call us $2*5$ rather than $(1 + 3i)*(1-3i)$.

The welfare state gives money to people who have not achieved anything others care to dignify with an income. This will not do. Much better to make bad loans to people who have been dignified with incomes drawn from other bad loans.

Beneath good and evil #965: the white woman's burden. -- She laughed to think how pathetically credulous her husband was to have swallowed that bilge she pledged at the altar. Luckily for him, her greatness of soul prevented her from dispelling his contemptible delusion.

Cash is a mark of approval; some people end up with a sheet full of gold stars the same way a frat boy wakes up with a drunken debutante.

While you were busy cleaning out your inbox that morning, the last moment elapsed when you might have been able to ignore the ravages of time on the face of a girl you have not seen in decades.

Boom and bust. Envy drives consumerism, but why would anyone with any remaining hopes of awakening love seek to awaken envy instead, and how long can anyone with no remaining hopes of awakening love be trusted to pay enough attention to this world to keep the money moving?

Show that your enemy's feigned modesty is real stupidity.

They were proud to be depicted as barely emerged from the collective unconscious. After all, how far could a person stray without becoming that worst of all evils, a homosexual?

The soldiers she believed herself entitled to despise as cannon fodder could just as easily have been sent to college as education fodder.

There are algebras where even though numbers have inverses there is no such thing as division: you can multiply x by the inverse of y, but if you multiply the result by y you do not get back to x. This is why divide and conquer so often goes astray.

If churches arise when a civilization has created too opaque a thicket of possible implications for the prole mind, then they are intellectual triage, and a very religious education is likely to amputate limbs there is no reason to suppose ignoble or gangrenous.

It is bad enough to discover you have given away your manufacturing secrets to the former barbarians overseas; the final indignity is the realization one has subcontracted one's memory to piddling scribes next door. The outsourcing of spirituality.

The core flaw of all competitive ideologies is their failure to recognize the point of diminishing returns. To the Yucatecs or Mongols or Syriacs or Shangs or Hittites, Claude Debussy might have been an immediately recognizable demigod, attended from his youth by swarms of apprentices and physicians, his acquaintance the Emperor's worthiest pleasure and greatest honor. It took the fantastic discipline and competitive sophistication of the Academy to miss the point entirely and waste mankind's time ridiculing him as an arpeggiator.

Our generation has witnessed cross-pollinations of mathematical physics and high finance so miraculous that they have transformed mindless proles into globe-straddling destroyers of antiquity's most priceless relics.

Half the claims in American politics amount to "I am the rightful owner of Central Park".

Repeating things that do not work is typically neurotic or insane. Repeating things that do work causes asset bubbles, typically neurotic or insane.

To find out how far a society has progressed in its cancer, ask how desperate it is to thwart secession. When a ruling class no longer has the wit to lead it hastens to settle for blank dominance.

Much of what commonly passes for maturity is a long resume of solutions to puzzles as self-contained and trivial as a newspaper acrostic.

He was well equipped to invent the wheel or the boat; to lead Israel out of Egypt, or spearhead the initial cultivation of the Amazon or the Yellow River Valley; to draft the Magna Carta, or the US Constitution; but he would never suspect it, because his visits to the casino had reduced him to debt slavery.

"Capital allocation typically proceeds more efficiently through the division of labor. A mind forced to juggle twenty balls will usually drop most of them, while ten minds can easily juggle two balls apiece. Therefore all capital allocation decisions must be removed from the public sphere and consolidated under my secret control." This masterpiece of narcissistic self-contradiction delighted the majority of voters. They sold the national highways, the Army, the Church and the Supreme Court to investors they proceeded to forbid themselves even to identify, let alone investigate. One day a burly armed man in sunglasses came to the house to inform them that because an anonymous government priest was dissatisfied with their surveillance transcripts they had been sold to an Arabian conglomerate. Farewell, homo rationis capax.

The sense of justice resembles the higher commutativity that allowed mankind to escape mighty Cayley's upper bound of 8 dimensions on division algebras. If you try to force intransitive operations on everyone you too will lose associativity and end up stuck in a fancy Flatland.

Civilization in five easy steps. Condemn yourself to a voyage across treacherous seas. Find a disagreeable virgin country to marry. Arrange a crushing defeat for yourself at the hands of barbarians. When you are back on your feet, tougher than ever, make sure they stick around to snipe at you night and day. Then get yourself persecuted, ostracized, or better yet, enslaved. After a workout like this you will have bigger intellectual biceps than Mr. Universe. Along the way you will have taken too many steroids so your testicles will eventually fall off.

Utopian militarism: two symptoms of decline for the price of twenty.

Some apparent lapses in creative power are merely interminable traffic jams caused by outside road construction. You forget you might be something other than an animal sitting exhaustedly in a hot iron box forever.

Denying that society is an organism is far from explaining how the analogy breaks down. A mass of people convinced it is fortunate enough to witness a novel form of self-actualization is more youthful than a mass accustomed to the same form as a banal fact of nature.

Every success tempts us to some fatal idolatry, some dimensionality reduction, but we cannot live without some success or other, so we go on reducing our dimensionality until the rats can nibble on us.

Each struggles for more than his share, and finally some succeed beyond redress; the demagogue and the profiteer manage to confiscate the cachet of the artist, morale becomes suboptimally distributed and the society falls apart.

Redistribution need have nothing to do with morality. Free-market economics depends on relatively rational actors and there is no real evidence that relative rationality can persist under catastrophic information overload. The essential thing is that redistributive actions are viscerally felt to be technical and unrelated to performance: i.e. a tax lottery.

Some illusions are like scabs and should not be removed; more are like blood poisoning that cannot.

If only the deaths we are able to arrange for ourselves met the standards for transfiguration.

A man tells you his murders will make the ballot box universal, but it turns out he was just a stooge mechanically acting out the ancient suicidal dream of Zerubbabel and Bar Kokaba, the dream of a universal Jewish empire. Do you get your money back? Do you get your dead auntie back? Or would that be 'antisemitic'?

Dominant classes want to be the only species left in the desert.

An emperor forced to employ mercenaries because of the scope of his holdings and the hardening of his vast frontier is at a comprehensible strategic impasse; but what can we say to excuse a politician who voluntarily switches from citizens to mercenaries, though he knows history's warning that they will turn on his republic? That he is not human enough to comprehend the scope of his betrayal?

Before you ridicule the idea of divine drugs, consider the Muselman-Sofi Hindu tradition of Mohammed's enlightenment. The prophet was out walking with Jabril when they stumbled across a party of forty buck naked souls. Because he was so courteous as to offer his white turban as a strainer for the bhang, they gave him some, and the angel of destiny escorted him through the eye of the needle into the secrets of Paradise.

Get lured into a boxing match and you end up a boggled boxer. The military-industrial complex which followed the defeat of Germany in the mid-twentieth century probably bankrupts the United States the same way the victory over the Achaemenians ruined Hellas.

What devil worthy of the name would extend suffering mankind a silver platter bearing instant relief from the appalling miscalculations of lust?

So long as the iron law of oligarchy is not broken and populations continue expanding to the limit of sustainability there can be no escape from the splitting of society into overclass and underclass, and the resultant degeneration of the provinces into militarism and decline. Hence random sortition and contraception are the pillars of any New World Order that deserves the name. You begin by decreeing that a small percentage of local and state bodies be selected as for jury duty.

Without certain coefficients the curves of life do not fit us, so when reason insists on using them to dissolve our equations into tautologies we are forced to bid it farewell.

Poor honest Mill thought that if you offered clever girls an intellectually level playing field they would all learn to disdain [ ]ing their way to the top. Instead we will live to see American parents hiring their sons tutors in the methods of the Russian secret services, in a desperate attempt to keep them abreast of the careerist whores.

Desire is intrinsically incoherent. Someone who believes in the power of prayer is lucky enough not to understand the problem of contradictory coefficient constraints.

Throw up your hands and vow to amuse yourself in your final weeks, and you will just end up watching the computation of a few more decimal places in the cosmic surd.

Psychedelics do jazz substitutions on neural progressions. When they meander too long among ten- and eleven-tone sonorities you are stuck with all the information paucity of one- and two-tone sonorities, plus the crushing overhead of seemingly endless dissonance.

The instruction manuals available for the organism always seem to fit similar but discontinued models instead.

Education: finding out that the most worthwhile things are things you can never be or have.

Gratitude has to go rancid when fate incessantly jeers at our efforts to repay our benefactors.

Aphorists and mathematicians share a vulnerability to sign errors. One of them along the way and you end up with glistening nothingness.

Dislike of abstraction varies directly with weakness for crude abstractions.

Op art is abstract geometry but abstract art is pragmatism run amok.

The noise the Impressionists added to visual signals seemed insipid to the Wild Beasts for the same reason basic sixth and seventh chord substitutions became insipid after decades of jazz. They wanted to see how far substitute-chord keys and blue notes could go without devastating diatonicism. Surrealism too was not really atonal; its abrupt changes of context were new key signatures, modal regions rather than chromatic totalitarianism.

Supermodels: the differential element is greater than the integral.

Zola's train roaring on into the night with a dead crew seems to symbolize industrial civilization, but the 'Budah Mimansa' says it symbolizes the entire material world.

In the early twentieth century every half idea promoted itself into an "ism"; who still bothers pretending to be a complete worldview?

Vox populi: Would you mind paying an enormous price to maintain my unconscious self-deception?

Revival of nineteenth-century academicism misses the point about the rise of photography. It is all very well to congratulate those who competed with the machine even at an unsustainable energy cost, but why condemn artists for proceeding to offer what the machine could not?

Some sin is merely fascination with permutations.

Everything exceptional shares the tragedy of heroin: what marriage could do justice to such a honeymoon?

Global interconnection fosters perceptual stasis, by robbing physical travel of its power to disrupt mental habits.

The totalitarian state can also be privatized.

We are varying boundary conditions on each other.

Every argument against cloning humans can be changed into an argument against us replicating at all.

People worry that the Third World will melt the atmosphere when it starts longing for manufactured goods. But what happens when the wretched of the earth become roués and start melting the intellectual world with their hunger for alienation effects?

The dominatrix explained that many of her clients had found their way into social niches where they were starved for useful feedback. No one dared offer them retail samples of free criticism, so they had to buy it wholesale.

Like the body, the mind will start devouring its muscle tissue without a modicum of external nourishment.

The Yekanahbinan sect envisioned the Trinity as recursive or fractal; recursion is the moral of the legend that the Divinity, as it began creation, attached Zarathustra's spirit to a tree symbolizing the primary intellect, its leaves all contingent existences. The First Intelligence formulated the Second Intelligence, the soul and the body of the upper heaven, and each of these conceived three further entities. The Parsees placed limits on the irreality of this infinite prism stack, but the Samradians denied that even divinity and ideality were more than mental categories.

Max Ball could not do a Cabaret Voltaire during our wars; everyone would show up with computers that would make the spectacles seem mundane.

Criticizing material interests is such serious business that today's election may have been won in solidarity against a remark a rabble-rouser made two hundred years ago.

An unconscious full of stale magic and mass-produced hallucination, casting the eerie light of a dying world on random scraps of trash paper, scandalizing only bores.

A critic with an indictment for each and every one of you.

Everything was a transference; the real problem could not even be stated. Last words: "We are meant to live a lie".

A personality like a vocoder, always expressing itself in parameter blips rather than fully developed curves.

Other people only stake marginal capital.

Our successes desert us; they are the work of someone else, someone who did not know their generality. Thirteen years after he himself had solved a first-order partial differential equation in three variables Lagrange was faced with one again and announced it was impossible with present methods.

Addiction is firm conviction that the alternatives are not real for you.

If your average moral song consisted of 5 diatonic triads you could spin 12!5 skits, each with 5! variants, each with a galaxy of orchestrations. Primitive opinion will always be foolishly outraged at people who cannot be satisfied with such an astronomical number of perms, and advanced opinion will always regret how many pleasures it will never stumble across in the wider universe.

Unlike junk food, journalism offers a mask of nimbleness to hide the obesity it causes.

The race is not yet intelligent enough for politicians to invent wholly imaginary enemies.

The multiplier effect formalizes ancient rules about pyramiding public morale with princely generosity.

An indisputable truth which any healthy brain would filter away as poisonous; the best-kept trade secret in history.

Pride places a decimal before others.

Why are we perfectly calm in the midst of disaster after throwing a tantrum at some triviality? What is intelligent about this design feature? -- A circuit breaker?

The Pythagorean theorem of political triangulation: the squares of competing truths sum to the square of the lie that conflates them.

Her neurotic need for superiority led her to trick the patient into abandoning his neurosis, his only weapon in the economic war with neurotics.

We are parodies of our higher selves.

Worldly wisdom is knowing when and how to admit truth has lost the round.

Infatuation fits the wrong curve to the beloved's data points. A straight line becomes a rosette and then the Witch of Agnesi.

Black and blue and red marble, curious ores, sapphires, rubies, chrysolites, corals and pearls, fabrics almost too lush to wear, perfumes and incense, lapis serpents, ancient tomes and paintings in need of restoration, divine mutants, silver laurels, dishes with a monstrous hint of sugar and asafetida, gold bricks and sandalwood, living statues of Venus, heated oils, human brains on green slabs, rainbow torches, herbs and gum arabic, four eagles on a throne, the glorious abandoned idols of some alien race, toppled across the floor of the platinum planetarium beneath the high lattice window.

www.ingramcontent.com/pod-product-compliance
Lightning Source LLC
Chambersburg PA
CBHW020514100426

42813CB00030B/3245/J